WILD WEST DAYS

WILD WEST DAYS

Discover the Past with Fun Projects, Games, Activities, and Recipes

David C. King

John Wiley & Sons, Inc.

New York • Chichester • Weinheim • Brisbane • Singapore • Toronto

Copyright © 1998 by David C. King
Illustrations © 1998 by Bobbie Moore
Published by John Wiley & Sons, Inc.

Design: Michaelis/Carpelis Design Assoc., Inc.

This publication is designed to provide accurate and authoritative information in regard to the subject matter covered. It is sold with the understanding that the publisher is not engaged in rendering legal, accounting, or other professional services. If legal advice or other expert assistance is required, the services of a competent professional person should be sought.

Library of Congress Cataloging-in-Publication Data
King, David C.
      Wild west days: discover the past with fun projects, games,
activities, and recipes / David C. King.
         p. cm.—(American kids in history series)
    Includes bibliographical references and index.
    Summary: Discusses what life was like for the people who settled
the West between 1870 and 1900, follows a year in the life of a
fictional family of that time, and presents projects and activities,
such as designing a brand stamp and making a yarn picture.
    ISBN 0-471-23919-4 (alk. paper)
    1.   Ranch life—West (U.S.)—Study and teaching—Activity programs-
-Juvenile literature. 2. West (U.S.)—Social life and customs-
-Study and teaching—Activity programs—Juvenile literature.
3.   Children—West (U.S.) —History—19th century—Study and teaching-
-Activity programs—Juvenile literature. [1. West (U.S.) —Social
life and customs. 2. West (U.S.)—History—19th century.
4. Frontier and pioneer life—West (U.S.)] I. Title. II. Series.
F596.K559 1998
978—dc21   97-48557

Printed in the United States of America
10 9 8 7 6 5 4 3 2 1

To Mom and Dad for the many years of
support and encouragement

ACKNOWLEDGMENTS

Special thanks to the many people who made this book possible, including: Kate C. Bradford, Joanne Palmer, and the editorial staff of the Professional and Trade Division, John Wiley & Sons, Inc.; Susan E. Meyer and the staff of Roundtable Press, Inc.; Marianne Palladino and Irene Carpelis of Michaelis/Carpelis Design; Miriam Sarzin, for her copy editing, Sharon Flitterman-King and Diane Ritch for craft expertise; Rona Tuccillo for picture research; Steven Tiger, librarian, and the students of the Roe-Jan Elementary School, Hillsdale, New York; and, for research assistance, the staff members of the Great Barrington Public Library, the Atheneum (Pittsfield, Massachusetts), Old Sturbridge Village, the Farmers Museum, Cooperstown, New York; and Nathan Bender of the Buffalo Bill Historical Center, Cody, Wyoming. Historical photographs courtesy of Dover Publications, Inc.

CONTENTS

INTRODUCTION

Moving West

Between the years 1870 and 1900, pioneers from the East and from Europe rapidly settled America's last western frontier, the lands between the Mississippi River and the Rocky Mountains. A railroad stretching all the way across the continent was completed in 1869, and other railroads soon followed. The last wave of pioneers could now travel in the comfort of a railroad car rather than by covered wagon.

Many of the late pioneers were farmers who plowed the thick grass of the prairie to plant large fields of wheat or corn. Other newcomers were miners, searching for gold and silver in the Rocky Mountains. Another group was made up of ranchers and cowboys. They drove huge herds of long-horned cattle north from Texas to the railroad lines. The cattle were then shipped by railroad to the East to provide meat for the nation's growing cities. Other settlers who had come to the Southwest even earlier were Spanish-speaking people who had settled the land when it was part of Mexico. By 1900, all of the western land had been formed into new states or territories that would soon become states.

Long before the pioneers came, the West had been home to dozens of Native American tribes, such as the Sioux and Cheyenne in the North and the Navaho, Hopi, and Apache in the

Southwest. As their lands were overrun by settlers, and the herds of buffalo were killed for their hides or for sport, some tribes fought fierce battles against the pioneers and the U.S. Army. But the tide of newcomers was too great, and by 1890 the army had forced all of the tribes onto special lands set aside for them called reservations.

For children growing up in those Wild West years, life was very different from anything they had known in the settled East or in Europe or China. They lived with a sense of excitement, adventure, and sometimes danger. Whether living in a town, on a farm, or on a ranch, both boys and girls worked hard as soon as they were old enough to help. Most young people also went to school, usually in a one-room schoolhouse where all ages learned together.

Children on farms and ranches were always thrilled by a trip into town. There they might meet other children from all parts of the country and from foreign countries as well. They could watch cattle being loaded onto railroad cars, or miners buying supplies. There were stores, restaurants, and sometimes an ice-cream parlor to visit. While town life was sometimes a little rowdy, there were not many of the gunfights that people back East read about in novels and magazines.

The Thayer Family

This book follows the story of the Thayer family during the year 1878. The Thayers were not a real family, but their story shows what life was like for people in the Wild West.

Joseph and Katherine Thayer had raised beef cattle in Virginia before they joined the westward movement with their children in 1875 so they could build a larger ranch on the inexpensive frontier lands. They traveled west by railroad to Wyoming Territory, where they bought land near the town of Cheyenne. Cheyenne was an important railroad stop, so they could easily ship their cattle to eastern markets.

The Thayer children and Mrs. Thayer stayed in a Cheyenne boarding house while Mr. Thayer worked with his hired hands to build a one-story ranch house. They also built a bunkhouse for the five hands, or cowboys, and for the ranch cook. Mr. Thayer signed a contract with a rancher in Texas for 2,000 head of cattle. He and the cowboys then rode to Texas to drive the herd north to the new ranch. By the summer of 1876, the family was living in their new home and the ranch was stocked with Texas longhorn cattle and about fifty horses.

In the spring of 1878, Tom Thayer was twelve years old and eager to become a full-fledged cowboy. His parents had promised that he could ride on part of a cattle drive later in the spring.

His sister Amy was a year younger than Tom and she, too, was thrilled by their new home. While Tom was eager to learn everything he could about cattle, Amy was more interested in the horses and was already an expert rider. When she wasn't in school or riding, Amy helped her mother and Miguel, the Mexican cook, prepare meals. The ranch hands ate with the family, so every meal required a lot of work. Tom also had regular chores, including having fresh horses ready for each of the cowboys and Pa.

The youngest in the family was Tad, who had just turned six. He would start school in the fall with Amy and Tom; the rest of the time, he was free to play.

The Projects and Activities

As you follow Amy, Tom, and Tad through the year 1878, you'll do many of the things children in the Wild West did. Like them, you'll learn some Native American activities, such as making a ceremonial shield, a gourd rattle, or a game called ring toss. You can also make ranch items or try recipes like ranch scrambled eggs or sourdough flapjacks.

As you do the recipes, projects, and activities, the past will come alive. And you'll discover what it was like to be growing up in the American Wild West.

CHAPTER ONE

SPRING

Spring was one of the busiest and most exciting seasons on the Thayer ranch. The longhorn cattle had wandered freely throughout the winter, and now it was time for the spring roundup. There were no fences around the Thayers' land, so many of the cattle could have wandered several miles through unowned land that was called the open range.

Pa Thayer and the five cowboys rode long distances every day for about two weeks, slowly moving the herd to grazing land closer to the ranch. They used their best horses for this work, horses that knew how to turn a steer that started to roam away from the others. If the steer bolted and ran, the cowboy rode swiftly after it and threw his lariat, or rope, over the steer's horns to stop it. Sometimes it was necessary to wrestle the steer to the ground to stop it. Once a steer had been roped, it usually quieted down and joined the rest of the herd.

BRANDING TIME

Once the herd was grazing closer to the ranch house, it was time for the most important part of the spring roundup—branding the new calves. Every ranch had its own brand, made out of iron, with a special design that identified the ranch. The branding iron was heated in a fire until it was red hot, then the cowboys stamped it on a calf, or on any unbranded steers they found. Branding hurt the calf only for a second, and from then on it wore the symbol of the ranch it belonged to.

Branding was hot, hard work that required speed and skill. One or two cowboys would "cut out" a calf from the herd by roping it, wrestling it to the ground, and quickly tying its hooves together. Another cowboy would then brand the calf. When it was let go, the calf scrambled to its feet and ran bawling and complaining back to its mother.

Amy and Tom were thrilled by the quick movements and sure

hands of the cowboys. And they were proud that this year they were allowed to help. Tom kept the branding irons hot, wearing the same thick gloves the cowboys wore. Amy helped the cook, Miguel, rub down the tired horses and bring fresh mounts to each cowboy whenever they were needed. Each cowboy and Pa changed horses every two or three hours.

PROJECT DESIGNING A BRAND STAMP

In this project, you'll create a design for a brand, very much like the designs ranchers used for their branding irons. You won't be branding calves, steers, or horses, but you can use your brand as an ink stamp to mark your books, note cards, or letters. You'll make your brand out of felt or chamois (SHA-mee) and a block of wood instead of metal. And, like the ranchers, you can start by trying out different designs with pencil and paper until you have one you like.

MATERIALS

pencil

paper

ruler

compass, or round object about 1½ inches in diameter

several sheets of newspaper

scrap of felt (any color) or chamois, about 6 inches square (available in the automotive department of most discount department stores and many supermarkets)

scissors

block of wood about 2 inches square and 1 inch high

craft glue or white glue

ink pad (available at stationery and office supply stores)

Rules for Designing a Brand

There were hundreds of different brand designs, but every brand was read in one of three ways:

1. From left to right. Sample: 2 – T means the "2 Bar T" brand.

2. From top to bottom. Sample: $\frac{\diamondsuit}{L}$ means "Diamond Bar L" brand.

3. From outside to inside. Sample: Ⓜ means "Circle M" brand.

Keep these rules in mind as you design your brand.

1. With pencil and paper, try different designs. You might use one or two of your initials, or a favorite number, and combine it with the symbols shown in the pictures. Other popular sym-

Texas Longhorn Cattle

In the early 1600s, Spanish settlers from Mexico brought cattle into what is now the state of Texas. Many of these long-horned animals wandered away from the Spanish *haciendas*, or ranches, and roamed wild in the semi-desert lands. Over the next 200 years, these wild herds grew larger and larger. By 1865, there were five million longhorns in Texas, most of them wild.

In the 1860s, a few ranchers came up with the idea of capturing some of the wild cattle, then moving them north to the railroad lines. The cattle could then be sold for shipment to eastern cities at a price of forty dollars or more each. The trail north was hard and dangerous. Bands of Native American warriors and cattle rustlers were a constant danger, but the profits were huge. In the 1870s, new ranches were started in Colorado and Wyoming. These northern ranchers mixed the tough longhorns with other breeds to produce better beef.

bols were a triangle, a box shape, or a heart. When you draw letters, use only capital letters. The design should measure about 1½ inches square, or across a circle.

2. Spread several sheets of newspaper over your work surface.

3. With the pencil, copy the design you like best onto the scrap of felt or chamois.

4. Carefully cut out the design pieces with scissors.

5. Place the block of wood flat on your work surface. Lay the design pieces on the block of wood backwards so that they will print correctly.

6. Use a pencil to trace around each piece of the brand design onto the wood block, so you will know where to glue each piece.

7. Spread glue evenly on the back of each piece of the design and press it into place on the block of wood. Let the glue dry.

8. You're now ready to use your brand just like a rubber stamp. Press the brand on the ink pad several times and then test it on a scrap of paper. Once the felt or chamois has absorbed a little ink, you can brand your books, notebooks, or other personal objects.

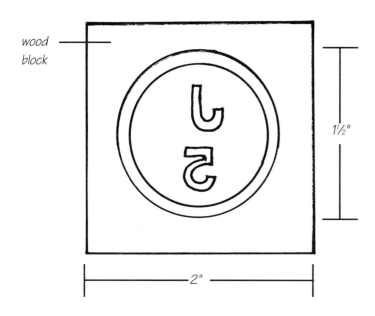

Circle J 2 brandblock

wood block

1½"

2"

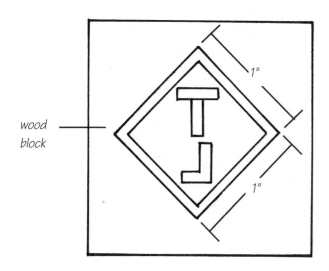

Diamond TL brand

wood block

1"

1"

PROJECT COWBOY MOBILE

Mobiles are easy—and fun—to make. Hang your cowboy mobile from the ceiling of your room and watch it move in the air currents.

MATERIALS

several sheets of newspaper
1 sheet of black poster board or cardboard, about 24 inches square
pencil
ruler
compass, or any round object about 4 inches in diameter
scissors
craft glue or white glue
hole punch
permanent black marking pen
strong black sewing thread or carpet thread
thin dowel 16 inches long
string
small metal screw-in hooks, such as a cup hook
adult helper

1. Spread several sheets of newspaper on your work surface, and lay the poster board flat on the newspapers.

2. On the poster board or cardboard, use light pencil to copy the drawings of the cowboy hat, bucking bronco, horseshoe, boot, and steer head. Make the drawings about as high and wide as shown in the picture.

3. When you are satisfied with your drawings, go over them with heavier pencil lines.

4. Copy the drawing of the brand on the poster board, making the circle about 4 inches in diameter. If you wish, you can use the brand design you made in the previous project—but adjust the drawing so that the numbers or letters reach to the sides of the circle, diamond, or other outside shape to make one piece.

5. Use scissors to cut out all the mobile shapes. For the brand, cut a thin piece for the circle or other border. Cut the numbers or letters as separate pieces, then glue them to the edge of the border, as shown in the picture.

6. With the hole punch, make holes in the cowboy hat, bucking bronco, boot, and steer head at the points shown in the picture.

7. Use black marking pen to cover the back of the poster board shapes (or both sides if you used cardboard).

8. Cut a piece of thread about 14 inches long. Tie one end to the dowel about 4 inches from the end. Allow about 12 inches of thread to the top of the boot. Run the thread through the hole in the top of the boot and tie it in a knot.

9. Cut a 6-inch piece of thread. Tie one end through the hole in the bottom of the boot, and the other end to the hole in the steer head.

10. Tie the cowboy hat and bucking bronco to the other end of the dowel in the same way, placing the thread about 4 inches from the end of the dowel. For these two shapes, use two pieces of thread about 12 inches long.

11. Tie the top of the brand to the center of the dowel with a 7-inch piece of thread.

12. Tie a short piece of thread between the ends of the horseshoe as shown in the picture. (The prongs of the horseshoe are pointed up for good luck.) Tie a 4-inch piece of thread from the bottom of the brand to the horseshoe thread.

13. Cut a 24-inch piece of string. Tie one end of the string to the dowel, about 2 inches from the end. Tie the other end of the string to the other end of the dowel. Squeeze a couple of drops of glue on the knots to hold them in place.

14. Your cowboy mobile is now ready to hang by a hook from your ceiling. Ask an adult to help you with this step.

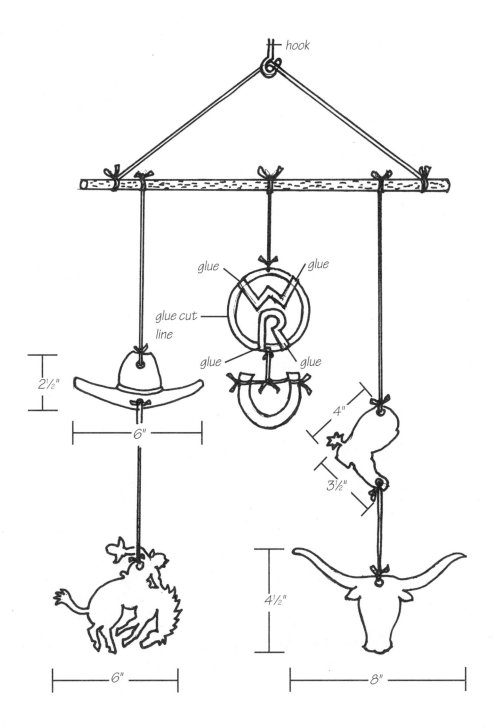

hook

glue   glue

glue cut line

glue   glue

2½"

6"

4"

3½"

4½"

6"

8"

The Cowboy's Equipment

The kinds of clothing and equipment American cowboys used were borrowed from the early Spanish cowboys who worked in present-day Texas and California. The cowboy's broad-brimmed hat protected him from sun or rain, and it was also useful as a pillow or for scooping up water to drink. Around his neck he wore a large bandanna, which he pulled up around his nose and mouth during dust storms. His boots had high heels to hold them in the stirrups firmly, and spurs to nudge the sides of the horse when speed was needed. Over his pants, the cowboy usually wore heavy leggings called chaps (SHAPS) for protection against thorny bushes and cacti. And for roping cattle, he used a braided leather or rawhide rope called a lariat, from the Spanish *la reata.*

Every cowboy carried a bag or pouch, called a poke, for carrying personal items like money, matches, tobacco and a pipe, and perhaps a deck of cards or a letter from a girlfriend. They attached these sacks to their belts with pieces of rawhide or stored them in a saddlebag. Pokes were usually made of hand-sewn leather, but you'll make a simpler version out of chamois, brown felt, or denim. Chamois cloth is soft hide, either real or synthetic, and can be found in the automotive section of most discount department stores and many supermarkets.

MATERIALS

several sheets of newspaper
6-by-20-inch piece of chamois, brown felt, or denim
masking tape
pencil
ruler
scissors
hole punch
rawhide lacing (sold as shoelaces), brown twine, or
*   jute, about 24 inches long*
fabric glue, white glue, or craft glue
stapler (optional)
small button
sewing needle and brown thread
permanent black marking pen or laundry marker

1. Spread several sheets of newspaper over your work surface.

2. Use 5 or 6 pieces of masking tape to hold the chamois flat and in place on your work surface. With pencil and ruler, draw a rectangle on the chamois or fabric, measuring about 6 inches wide and 19 inches long.

3. Mark a dot in pencil 2 inches in from each side of the fabric at the top edge. Mark two more dots 3 inches down each side edge. Connect the two dots in pencil on each side to create the flap shape shown in the picture.

4. Cut out the pattern with scissors.

5. Use the hole punch to make 2 holes in B, about 1 inch in from the sides, as indicated in the picture.

6. With scissors, cut a small buttonhole slit in the flap as shown. Make the slit just long enough for the button to fit through easily.

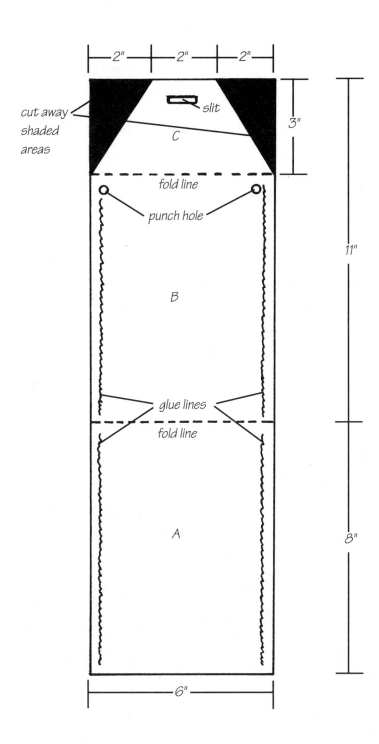

cut away shaded areas

2" 2" 2"

slit

C

3"

fold line

punch hole

B

11"

glue lines

fold line

A

8"

6"

7. Spread glue evenly along the sides of A and B, as shown by the wavy lines. Fold A 8 inches onto B and press firmly in place. Keep pressing the edges of A to B as the glue dries—about 5 minutes. *Optional: To reinforce the seam, you can put about 6 staples down each side.*

8. Tie a double knot at one end of the rawhide lacing or twine. Thread the other end all the way through one of the holes in B so that the knot is inside the pouch.

9. Thread the other end of the lacing through the back of the other hole in B and tie another double knot. The two knots will hold the lacing in place so that you can carry the poke pouch over your shoulder.

10. Fold the flap over and make a pencil mark through the slit onto A to mark where the button will be placed.

11. Cut a piece of brown thread about 12 inches long. Thread it through the eye of the needle, then tie the ends in a double knot.

12. Starting from inside the bag, push the needle through the cloth where you made the pencil mark and through a hole in the button. Then sew down through another hole and through the fabric.

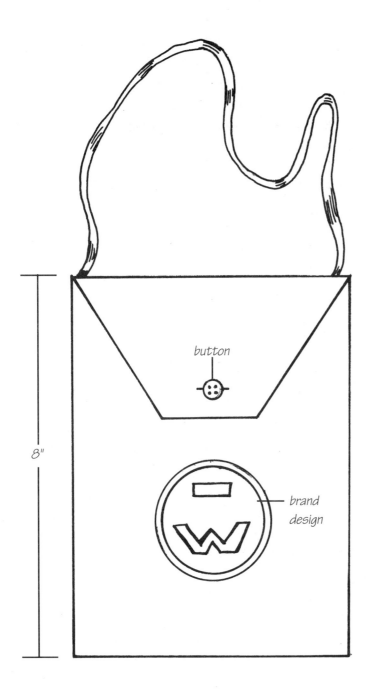

button

brand
design

8"

13. Continue sewing until the button is firmly attached. Cut the thread and tie the ends in a tight knot against the fabric. To close the poke pouch, just slip the button through the slit in the flap.

14. With marking pen or laundry marker, copy your brand design—or invent a new one—onto the front of the pouch below the flap. Your poke pouch is now ready to hold some of your light-weight personal items. *Note*: Even with staples to reinforce the seams, your poke pouch is not designed for heavy use. To make seams for heavy use, ask an adult to help you sew the seams on a sewing machine.

ROUNDUP RECIPES

The days of rounding up and branding the cattle produced wild scenes of whirling lariats, pounding hooves, bellowing cattle, shouting cowboys, clouds of dust, and broiling sun. Amy and Tom loved the action and excitement, and even the cowboys would pause to watch one of the men ride down a troublesome steer or calf. There were funny moments, too, especially when a frisky calf managed to escape capture again and again.

Pa and the cowboys started work at dawn, while the air was still cool. This meant that Ma, the cook Miguel, and Amy had to fix breakfast by the light of kerosene lamps at four in the morning. The men's favorite breakfast was steak and sourdough flapjacks served with cup after cup of strong coffee flavored with canned milk and sugar. The five cowboys often had contests to see

who could eat the most flapjacks, and Amy was amazed at how many they could consume. The men were thirsty and hungry throughout the hot day, so Miguel made large pitchers of his special fruit punch.

PROJECT SOURDOUGH STARTER

Cowboys on the trail and miners roaming the mountains carried a special mixture called sourdough starter to use in place of yeast for baking and cooking. Yeast is made up of organisms that give off a gas that makes dough rise. Miners in the West ate so much sourdough bread that all miners became known as "sourdoughs." To make sourdough flapjacks in the next project, you should plan to make sourdough starter about five days ahead. Check cookbooks at home or in the library to find other things you can use your starter to make, like sourdough biscuits or bread.

INGREDIENTS

½ cup lukewarm tap water
1 package active dry yeast
1 tablespoon sugar
2 cups warm tap water
2½ cups all-purpose flour

EQUIPMENT

measuring cup
measuring spoons
medium-size mixing bowl
mixing spoon
candy thermometer (optional)
large glass jar (a 2-quart canning jar works well)
paper towel
rubber band

MAKES

enough starter for 4 or 5 recipes

1. Measure ½ cup of lukewarm water into the mixing bowl. Stir in the yeast and continue stirring gently until all the yeast has dissolved.

2. Add the sugar and stir to dissolve it.

3. Stir in the 2 cups of warm water. *Note: If the water is too hot, it will kill the yeast. You can test the water first with a candy thermometer to make sure you have a temperature between 105 and 115°F, or just use your finger to guess that the water is slightly warmer than your body's temperature. Wait for the yeast to bubble to show that it's working.*

4. Slowly add the flour, stirring constantly to prevent lumps. Stir the mixture well until it is smooth.

5. Pour the mixture into the glass jar and place a single sheet of paper towel over the top.

6. Let the jar stand in a warm place for at least three days until bubbles form. Aging the starter this way can take up to five days, so don't be discouraged if no bubbles have formed by the third day. Stir the mixture twice a day during the aging. Once the bubbles have formed, your starter is ready to use.

7. Store the starter until you're ready to use it by fastening the paper towel over the jar top with a rubber band. You can store it in the refrigerator for up to two weeks.

PROJECT SOURDOUGH FLAPJACKS

Sourdough flapjacks are much like regular pancakes, but with the special sourdough flavor. Serve them with butter and maple syrup. Or, instead of syrup, try honey, powdered sugar, or jam. Cowboys often used molasses, and you might want to try that as well. The flapjacks come out best if you follow steps 1 to 4 the night before.

INGREDIENTS

1 cup sourdough starter (from previous project)
1 can evaporated milk
½ cup water
2 cups flour
3 eggs
2 tablespoons sugar
½ teaspoon salt
½ teaspoon baking soda
1½ teaspoons baking powder
1 to 2 tablespoons cooking oil
butter and maple syrup, honey, powdered sugar, or jam

EQUIPMENT

measuring cup
2 mixing bowls, 1 large and 1 small
mixing spoon
clean dish towel
measuring spoons
pancake griddle or large frying pan
waxed paper
pancake turner
adult helper

Horses: The Roundup Experts

Every cowboy on a ranch was assigned five or six horses, in addition to his own, if he had one. The horses prized above all others were called cutting horses. Years of training and experience gave cutting horses a special skill for cutting out, or separating, a steer or calf from the herd. The cowboy had to do little more than show the horse which animal to cut out, and the horse took over. Moving swiftly and carefully, the horse maneuvered the animal away from the others, blocking every move the steer or calf tried to make. A steer could be extremely dangerous if it charged, so a good cutting horse was a great friend for even the best cowboy.

MAKES

about 4 servings, or about 32 "silver dollar" pancakes

1. The night before you plan to have sourdough flapjacks, place sourdough starter into a large mixing bowl.

2. Stir in the evaporated milk and water.

3. Slowly add the flour, stirring constantly until there are no lumps.

4. Cover the bowl with a clean dish towel and let it stand at room temperature overnight.

5. In the morning, break the eggs into the small mixing bowl and beat them well with a mixing spoon.

6. Ask your adult helper to heat the pancake griddle on the stove.

7. While the griddle heats up, add the eggs, sugar, salt, baking soda, and baking powder to the batter. Stir it well until it's smooth.

8. The griddle is hot enough when a drop of water bounces on the surface. Pour 1 tablespoon of cooking oil on the griddle.

9. Have an adult use a folded-up piece of waxed paper to spread the oil evenly.

10. Have the adult help you pour about 2 tablespoons of batter on the griddle for each flapjack. Cook three or four at a time.

11. Bubbles will appear on the top of the pancakes. When the bubbles start to break, flip the flapjacks over with the turner. Cook the other side until golden brown. Serve hot with butter and the topping of your choice.

PROJECT RANCH-STYLE FRUIT PUNCH

Ranch cooks made a variety of cold fruit drinks. Citrus fruits, like lemons, limes, and oranges, were favorite ingredients because they were great thirst quenchers and they also prevented a common disease called scurvy. (Scurvy is caused by not having enough vitamin C and leads to bleeding gums and loss of strength.) Citrus fruits were shipped by railroad from citrus groves in California. The fruits were so highly prized on the frontier that it was not unusual for miners, farm families, or ranchers to pay a dollar for a single lemon.

INGREDIENTS

½ cup water
¼ cup sugar
1 cup orange juice
1 cup grape juice
¼ cup lime or lemon juice
1 orange, lemon, or lime
2 cups club soda
ice

EQUIPMENT

measuring cup
small saucepan
mixing spoon
cutting board
paring knife (to be used by an adult)
1½-quart pitcher
adult helper

MAKES

about 4 10-ounce servings

1. Measure ½ cup water into a small saucepan.

2. Ask your adult helper to heat the water until it starts to boil, then turn off the heat.

3. While the water is still hot, stir in the sugar. Keep stirring until the sugar has dissolved.

4. Pour the orange juice, grape juice, and lime or lemon juice into the pitcher.

5. Have an adult help you cut a lemon, lime, or orange into thin slices. Add the slices to the juices.

6. When the sugar water has cooled, pour it into the pitcher and stir well to blend all the ingredients.

7. Store the pitcher in the refrigerator until you're ready to serve it. Chill the club soda, too.

8. Just before serving, add the soda. Stir. Pour into tall glasses. Add ice cubes.

 **BEEF JERKY**

Whether riding the range or on a cattle drive, cowboys liked to carry a little food with them. Dried fruit and dried beef, or jerky, were favorite portable foods because they didn't spoil. Americans on the frontier learned to make jerky from the Sioux, Blackfoot, and other Plains Indian tribes. Native American women made jerky by cutting deer, elk, or buffalo meat into thin strips and hanging it from poles to dry in the sun or over a smoky fire. After several days, the jerky was ready and would remain unspoiled for months. Ranchers and cowboys liked to have the beef salted or rubbed with garlic for added flavor. Rather than curing the meat outdoors, you'll dry your beef jerky in the oven. You'll need to start the night before by putting the meat in a marinade to soak.

INGREDIENTS

1 pound lean flank steak or round steak
½ cup soy sauce
¾ cup water
1 teaspoon salt or seasoned salt
¼ teaspoon pepper
½ teaspoon garlic salt
½ teaspoon sage
*1 teaspoon liquid smoke (optional, available in the
   barbecue section of most supermarkets)*

EQUIPMENT

measuring cup
measuring spoons
medium-size mixing bowl
mixing spoon
meat cutting board
sharp knife and meat fork (to be used by an adult)
several paper towels
*aluminum foil broiling pan, or regular roasting pan
   and aluminum foil*
1-quart glass or plastic storage container
adult helper

MAKES

4 to 6 snack servings

1. Place the meat in the freezer compartment for about an hour to make it easier to cut.

2. While the meat is chilling, make a sauce for marinating: Put soy sauce into the mixing bowl. Add the water, salt, pepper, garlic salt, sage, and liquid smoke to the soy sauce. Stir the mixture well to blend all the ingredients.

3. Remove the steak from the freezer and place it on a cutting board. Ask an adult to help you cut the steak into thin strips, ¼ to ½ inch wide. Cut out any fat.

4. Place the beef strips in the bowl of marinade. Store in the refrigerator overnight.

5. After marinating, pour off the mixture and pat the beef strips dry on paper towels.

6. Preheat the oven to 150°F. Place a layer of beef strips in a broiling pan about ½ inch apart. Make a second layer of strips at right angles to the first layer, in a criss-cross pattern. *Note*: If you use a regular roasting pan, place a sheet of aluminum foil in the bottom of the pan. Fold the foil into ridges to allow the juice to run off.

7. Bake the beef strips for about 6 hours, or until the meat is completely dry. (If a strip breaks when you bend it, instead of folding, it is plenty dry.)

8. Allow your beef jerky to cool for at least an hour. Sample a piece or two and store the rest in a lightly covered glass or plastic container. The jerky will not spoil for several weeks.

Native American Pemmican

Plains tribes like the Sioux used dried buffalo meat, or jerky, to make a favorite food called pemmican. Sioux women made pemmican by pounding the jerky with a smooth rock until it became a powder. They then added ground-up seeds, dried fruits, and nuts. They soaked the mixture in melted animal fat; when the fat cooled, it held the pemmican together. A half-pound ball of pemmican provided a hunter or traveler with enough nourishment for an entire day. Native Americans usually stored large amounts of pemmican for the winter months when hunting was more difficult. The meat remained edible for a year or more. Pemmican is still popular today with backpackers and hunters.

NEW MEXICO ADVENTURE

Early in May, when the spring roundup was finished, Tom set off for New Mexico Territory with Kip, the ranch's African American cowboy. They planned to meet a large cattle drive coming north from Texas that included 200 more longhorns for the Thayer ranch. Tom's heart pounded with excitement as they headed south, leading the eight horses they would need on the cattle drive.

Kip was much older than the other four cowboys, who were all in their early twenties. He had escaped from slavery in 1858, a few years before the Civil War (1861–1865) finally brought slavery in America to an end. After making his way to the western frontier, Kip had become a cowboy. By 1878, he had taken part in nearly twenty spring roundups.

Tom and Kip rode through Colorado to the trading post of Taos, New Mexico. While they waited for the cattle drive, Kip and Tom visited nearby Native American Zuni villages. Tom was fascinated by the Acoma and Zuni dwellings, called *pueblos*, made of stone covered with sun-dried mud, or *adobe*. Several families lived in each pueblo, and some of the buildings were four stories high. They saw Zuni children playing games, including one called ring-in-a-ring, and watched Acoma women making beautiful pottery bowls. Tom couldn't wait to show Amy and Tad how to play ring-in-a-ring and how to make clay bowls when they got back home.

PROJECT PAINTED ACOMA BOWL

Most Native American tribes used clay to make pottery bowls, jugs, plates, and cooking pots. The pottery of the Pueblo tribes of the Southwest, like the Acoma, Hopi, and Zuni, are among the most famous for their beautiful designs. Each tribe had its own techniques and designs, but each potter added his or her own artistic touch. In this project, you'll make and decorate a clay bowl, using a method much like the one still used by Acoma women today. Instead of using regular clay that has to be fired in a special oven called a kiln, you can make your bowl out of self-hardening clay. Self-hardening clay is available in the craft or toy section of most discount department stores.

MATERIALS

several sheets of newspaper

waxed paper, about 2 feet

masking tape

1 1-pound package of self-hardening clay

table knife

glass or other round object about 4 inches in diameter

ruler

craft stick or clay-modeling tool

pencil

poster paints or acrylic paints: reddish brown, black, yellow

small paintbrush

acrylic varnish (optional) Note: acrylic varnish is not oil-based and is perfectly safe to use. Spray cans are not recommended, however.

small brush for varnish (optional)

1. Spread several sheets of newspaper on your work surface. Place a large sheet of waxed paper on top of the newspaper and fix it in place with masking tape. This will keep the clay from becoming smudged with newspaper ink.

2. Open the package of clay and knead the clay with your fingers to make it soft and easy to form.

3. Use a table knife to cut off a little less than one-half of the piece of clay. Form this piece into a rough ball shape.

4. Flatten the ball with the heel of your hands and your fingers to make a flat, round pancake shape between ¼ and ½ inch thick.

5. Press a glass or other round object into the clay pancake to make a circle about 4 inches in diameter. (Diameter is a line running through the center of a circle from one side to the other.) Remove the clay circle and add the scraps to your remaining chunk of clay.

Pueblo Pottery

The Pueblo tribes of the Southwest have always made their pottery without potter's wheels—wheels that make it easy for a potter to shape perfectly round forms. Before the Europeans arrived in North America, Native American peoples did not know about wheels of any kind—for wagons, for grinding grain, or for making pottery.

Even without potter's wheels, the Pueblo potters make beautifully shaped bowls and jugs. The potters, mostly women, traditionally used scraps of gourd as tools and they polished the pots with a smooth stone. They hardened the pottery by placing it over a bed of coals, with dried sheep manure on top. This method produced a fire so hot that the pots hardened in less than two hours. Modern Native American potters in New Mexico and Arizona continue this outstanding craft tradition, although many now use modern tools and kilns.

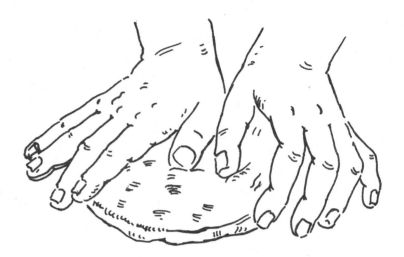

6. To make the wall of the bowl, break off a small piece of clay and press it to the edge of the circle base. Continue with more small pieces all the way around the base, as shown in the picture.

7. Build the wall as high as you wish by adding more small pieces all the way around.

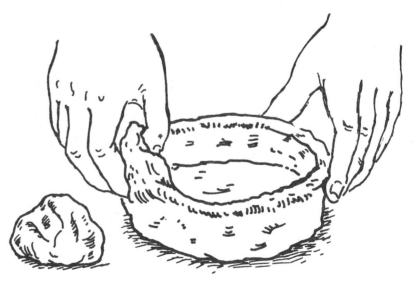

8. Use a craft stick or other modeling tool to make all the surfaces as smooth as possible.

9. Allow the clay to dry completely. Drying times vary, so follow the directions on the package. If you're not sure, let the bowl dry overnight.

10. Draw a design on the outside wall of the bowl in pencil—on the inside, too, if you wish. You can copy the design shown in the picture or invent your own.

11. Paint the design with reddish brown, black, and yellow paint. These are common Acoma colors that the women made from ground-up plants and minerals. Allow the paint to dry for an hour or two.

12. To give the bowl the polished look of Acoma pottery, apply one or two coats of acrylic varnish, with a different brush from the one used for paints. Allow the varnish to dry for about an hour between coats.

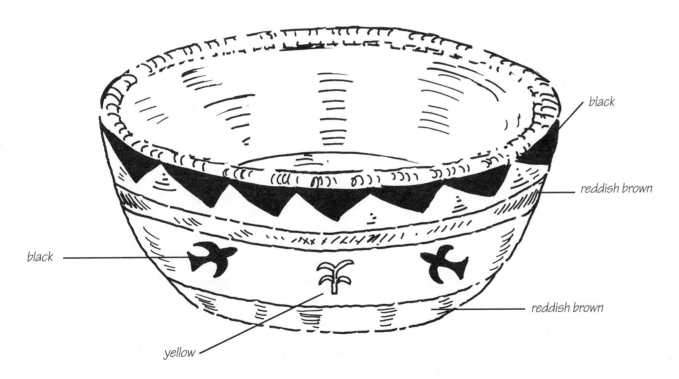

black

reddish brown

black

yellow

reddish brown

 ## ZUNI RING-IN-A-RING GAME

Many Native American games helped children learn and practice skills they would need as adults. Games for boys, for example, included running, throwing, or aiming a spear or dart, useful in real life for hunting animals. A favorite game in the Southwest was one the Zuni people called *Tsi-ko-Wai*—tossing a small ring inside a larger one. You'll discover that it takes a good deal of practice and skill to make a perfect toss. Zuni children made the rings by bending willow branches into a circle, then wrapping them with yarn. To make your version of this challenging game, you'll use rope instead of willow branches. (Of course, if you have a willow tree nearby, you can use two short branches.) The game can be played indoors or out, with two players, or with teams of two.

MATERIALS
ruler
rope or clothesline, at least 33 inches
scissors
adhesive tape, about 8 inches
pencil
about 10 inches of blue yarn, 10 inches of green, and
*   14 to 16 inches of white*
white glue or craft glue

2 players or 2 teams

1. Measure and cut with scissors a 20-inch length of clothesline or other rope.

2. Form a circle with the rope. At the point where the ends meet, wrap about 4 inches of adhesive tape around the rope to hold the circle closed.

3. Repeat steps 1 and 2 with a 13-inch length of rope.

4. With ruler and pencil, divide the larger ring into four quarters: Lay the ruler across the center of the ring to divide the ring in half; make a pencil mark on the ring at either end of the ruler. Place the ruler across the other half circle, and make two more pencil marks. The four marks create four equal quarters.

5. Tie a piece of blue yarn around one pencil mark, and wind the yarn tightly around the ring to the next pencil mark, as shown in the picture. When you reach the end of the quarter section, tie the yarn in a firm double knot, and cut off the extra yarn.

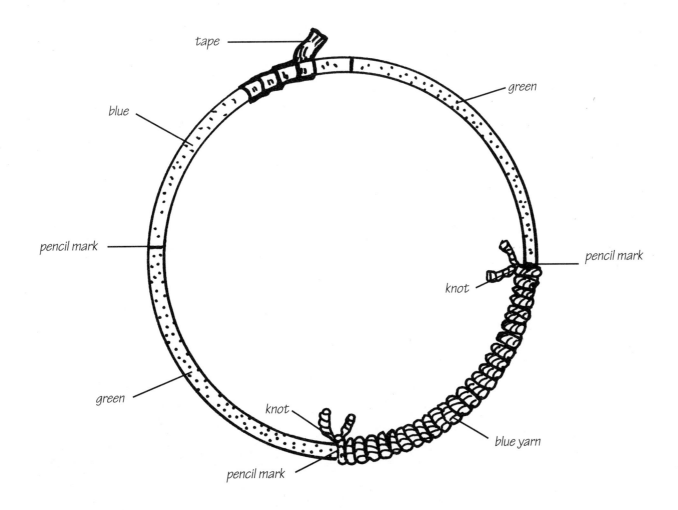

tape

blue

pencil mark

green

green

knot

pencil mark

knot

pencil mark

blue yarn

6. In the same way, wrap the next section in green yarn, the third in blue, and the final quarter in green, as indicated in the picture.

7. Place a couple of drops of glue on each of the knots to help hold them in place.

8. Wrap the smaller ring in white yarn.

9. Mark a tossing line to stand behind with stones or any other handy objects. Place the large ring on the ground at a distance of 10 to 15 feet from the tossing line.

10. The first player (or team) has three tosses, trying to toss the white ring inside the blue-green ring. The second player (or team) then has three tosses.

11. Scoring

- white ring completely inside, not touching any blue or green: 3 points
- any part of the white ring touching green: 1 point
- a miss, or touching blue and no green: 0 points.

12. Keep taking turns until one player or team scores 10 points. In case of a tie, the next toss determines the winner.

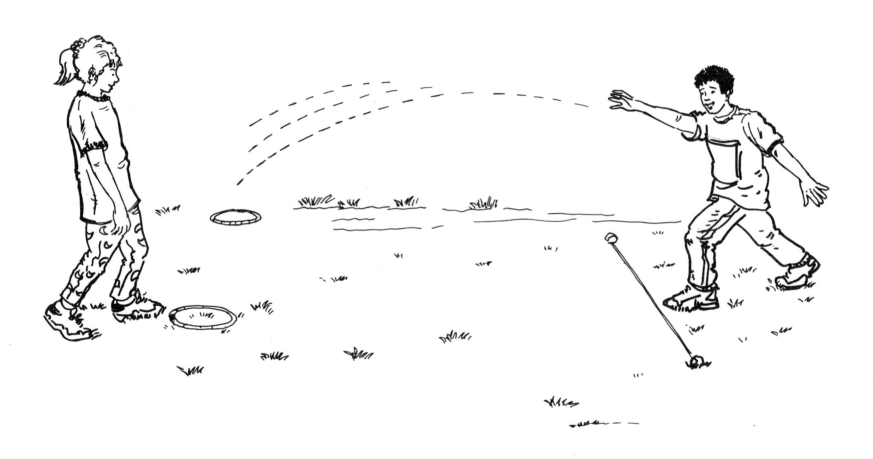

PROJECT MODEL PUEBLO

Southwestern tribes like the Hopi and Zuni made their pueblos out of stone covered with adobe. They used heavy logs for roof beams, laid smaller branches across the beams, and then plastered the roof and ceiling with adobe. Ladders were used to reach the upper stories, and the roof of one story formed a terrace for the family living above. The home on each level contained several rooms that remained cool in summer and were easy to heat in winter because the adobe kept them well insulated. In the plaza in front of each pueblo, the women baked bread in large beehive-shaped ovens that the Spanish settlers called *hornos*. In this project, you'll use easy-to-find materials to make a model of a pueblo.

MATERIALS
several sheets of newspaper
3 or 4 small cardboard boxes of different sizes
beige or light tan poster paint
paintbrush, ½ to 1 inch wide
1 cup yellow cornmeal or sand
pencil
ruler
black marking pen
nail or compass point
*18 to 20 thin, straight twigs or a thin dowel (you'll
    need a total of 36 inches or more)*

scissors
white glue
¼ to ½ pound self-hardening clay
adult helper

1. Spread several sheets of newspaper on your work surface. Arrange the boxes on the newspaper, one on top of the other, with the largest on the bottom, the smallest on top.

2. Paint the sides and tops of all the boxes with light tan or beige paint. While the paint is still wet, sprinkle a little yellow cornmeal or sand on all surfaces to give them the look of adobe. Allow the paint to dry for at least an hour.

3. With pencil and ruler, mark door openings and several windows on each level. (Notice that doors and windows in a pueblo are quite small.) Mark a small opening in one corner of each roof as a chimney hole.

4. Color the door, windows, and chimney holes with black marker.

5. Use a nail or compass point to make four or five holes through the front and back of each box near the roof of each level.

6. Place a 1-inch piece of dowel or twig about halfway through each hole to create the roof beams. Thin dowels and twigs can usually be cut with scissors; if this doesn't work, ask the adult to help you cut the pieces. Fix each beam in place with a little glue.

7. Use dowels or twigs to make a ladder for each level. Glue the short rungs of the ladder to the sides. The length of each ladder will depend on the height of the boxes.

8. Use self-hardening clay to make two or three *hornos* to place in front of your pueblo. You can also make clay figures and small bowls or jugs to complete the scene.

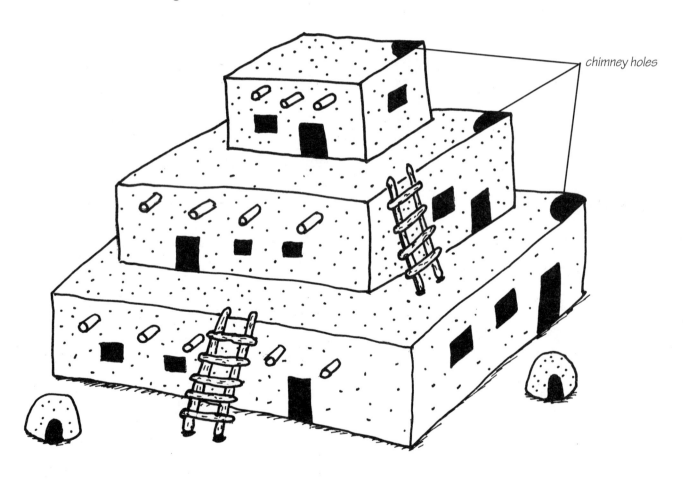

chimney holes

CHAPTER TWO

SUMMER

Late in May, Tom and Kip met the cattle drive near Taos and spent the next six weeks on the trail. Tom was amazed at the size of the herd. There were more than 2,000 longhorns, with a crew of nine cowboys, the trail boss, a cook, and a wrangler who took care of the horses. When they were on the move, the herd stretched out for more than a mile, stirring up great clouds of dust.

While Kip rode with the cowboys, Tom was proud when the trail boss told him he would ride as a wrangler. He worked with the outfit's regular wrangler, a fourteen-year-old boy named Will. The two boys were in charge of more than sixty horses needed on the drive, since each cowboy changed horses several times a day. The band of horses was called the "saddle band" or the *remuda*, from the Spanish word for "change" or "replacement."

ON THE TRAIL

As the cowboys moved the herd slowly north at the rate of ten or twelve miles a day, Tom learned about the hardships of a cattle drive. In addition to rainstorms, dust storms, and broiling sun, he discovered how hard it was to be in the saddle sixteen hours a day.

There were dangers, too, especially the danger of a stampede. The slightest noise or a flash of lightning could send a herd into a wild frenzy that would take the cowboys hours, or even days, to bring under control.

The cook always rode ahead of the drive to set up his chuck wagon at the next stopping place. Tom found that mealtimes were most welcome, for the rest as well as the food. He especially liked soaking up the steak or bacon drippings with fresh-baked biscuits. The cook gave him dried fruit, called fruit leather, to eat between meals. Whenever he could, Kip taught him such things as how to find direction with his pocketwatch in case he became lost, and how to measure the distance across a stream or river.

PROJECT FINDING DIRECTION

When you're trying to find compass directions (north, south, east, west), you only need to find one in order to figure out the other three. If you can find which direction is south, for example, you know that north is behind you, east is on your left, and west is on your right. Here is a simple way to find direction using only a watch and a stick. Cowboys used methods like this because they rarely carried a compass.

MATERIALS

small, straight stick
watch or portable clock
compass (optional)

1. Find a patch of level ground and poke the stick into the ground. Make sure the stick is straight up and down.

2. If the watch or clock is set to daylight savings time, move it back one hour to standard time. Place the watch next to the stick so that the sun's shadow on the stick falls exactly across the hour hand.

3. Find the spot halfway between the hour hand and twelve. A line from the center of the watch through that spot points south. For example, if the shadow falls across the hour hand at 10:00 o'clock, the spot at 11:00 points south.

4. You can check your results with a compass. The needle of the compass should fall along the same line but pointing north.

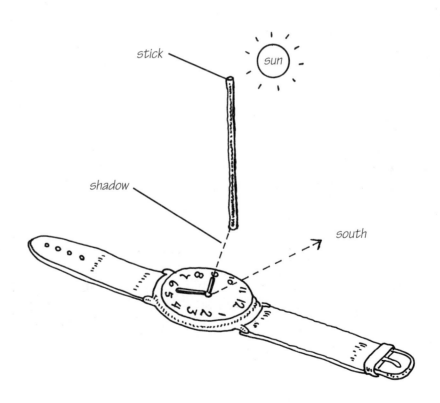

PROJECT: MEASURING DISTANCE

One of the many challenges of travel on the western frontier was finding the best way to cross rivers and streams. Leaders of pioneer wagon trains and trail bosses on cattle drives looked for a crossing place that was shallow and the shortest possible distance across. The inventive Westerners developed different methods for measuring across a river. Once they knew the distance, they could tell how long a guide rope was needed to stretch across. The guide rope helped keep people or animals from drifting downstream with the current. They also often used ropes to pull wagons, people, or reluctant animals across.

In this activity, you can try two of the methods people used on the frontier. For both methods, find a place outdoors that will be your "river" to measure across. This could be a pond, a vacant lot, someone's yard, or part of a playground.

Method 1: Hat-Brim Measurment

This method of measuring distance probably began during the Civil War. Army officers simply used the brim of their hats to get a rough reading of distance, comparing it to a similar distance on land by pacing it off. You can try exactly the same technique.

MATERIALS

open space outdoors to serve as the "river"
hat with a brim, or cap with a peak (like a baseball cap)
ruler, yardstick, or tape measure
pencil
paper
helper

1. Choose a rock, tree, post, or any other object on the other side of your "river" as a marker to measure to. Imagine that the current is flowing from left to right, as shown in the picture. If you measure your crossing from point A to point B, rather than C to B, the current will help people and animals cross; they won't have to fight against the current.

2. Place the hat or cap on your head. Stand at point A, lower your chin a little, and fix your gaze on the distant marker.

3. Move your chin up or down until the peak of your cap seems to touch the marker.

4. Keep your head in exactly the same position, with your chin lowered or rasied. Turn to the side and look along your side of the river. Ask your helper to move to a spot where your cap peak seems to touch her feet.

5. The distance from you to your helper is about the same as the distance across the river. To measure this in feet, use a ruler, yardstick, or tape measure to determine the length of one of your steps or strides. Write down the number of inches on a piece of paper.

6. Pace off the distance from your spot to your helper. If each of your steps measured 15 inches and you took 20 steps, the distance would be 20 x 15 = 300 inches, or 25 feet. Use pencil and paper to work out your actual measurements. Try the next method and see which is more accurate.

Method 2: Triangulation

Triangulation sounds complicated, but it isn't—it simply means using triangles to make measurements. Surveyors, people who measure land, use this method today to make sure their measurements are accurate.

MATERIALS

open space outdoors to serve as the "river"
3 dowels, straight sticks, or garden stakes, about 1
  foot long (all three must be exactly the same
  length)
4 small pegs (scraps of wood or pencils)
ball of string
tape measure
pencil
paper
helper

1. Choose a rock, tree, or other marker on the far side of the "river" to measure to. On the diagram, this will be point D.

2. Lay the 3 dowels or sticks on the ground on your side of the river and form them into a triangle. Position the triangle so that side AB is lined up with point D, as shown in the diagram.

3. Firmly stick 3 pegs in the ground at the three points of the triangle. Once the pegs are in place, remove the dowels or sticks.

4. Tie one end of the ball of string to the peg at point A. Stretch the string past point C and keep stretching it toward point G in a straight line. Point G is the spot where you think you are about the same distance from point D as you were at point A. You can have a helper hold the string at the peg so that the peg doesn't pull loose.

5. Move along the straight string line AG and set up your triangle again. This time, sides EG must line up with point D. Move the triangle to the left or right until you have a perfect lineup.

6. Put the fourth peg in the ground at point G. Tie the other end of the string to this peg. (You don't have to cut the string; you can roll up the ball later.) As you can see by the dotted lines in the diagram, you've created one large triangle, ADG, that has the same shape as triangles ABC and EFG. (Because all sides of these triangles are equal, they are called equilateral triangles.)

7. Since the current in the diagram is moving from left to right, the best way to cross is from point A to point D, so that the current will help in the crossing. How far is it? It's the same distance as your string line from point A to point G, because all sides of the triangle are the same length.

8. Use a tape measure to find the distance in feet from point A to point G. If the string is 32 feet long, then the distance across the stream from point A to point D is also 32 feet. How does the result compare to the hat-brim method? (You can measure the actual distance with the tape measure—unless, of course, you were measuring across an actual body of water.)

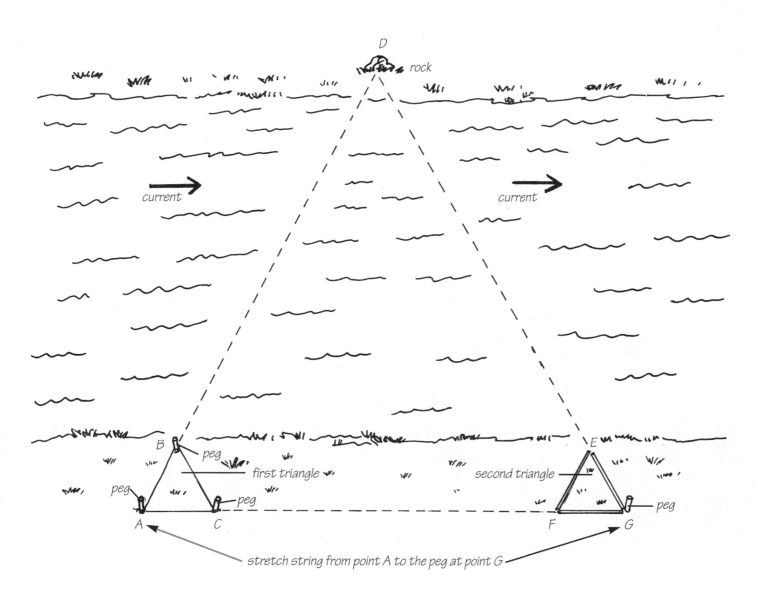

D

rock

current

current

B

peg

first triangle

peg

peg

second triangle

E

peg

A

C

F

G

stretch string from point A to the peg at point G

The Great Cattle Drives

The long cattle drives from Texas north to the railroad lines went on for only about 20 years, from the late 1860s to the late 1880s. For about 3 months each year, cowboys faced the hard, dangerous job of guiding the huge herds of longhorns. Bands of Native American warriors or cattle rustlers sometimes stampeded a herd in order to catch strays, although they rarely attacked the cowboys themselves. The only way the cowboys could stop a stampede was to race ahead of the leaders and turn them into a circle. They made the circle smaller and smaller until the cattle became tired and finally stopped. Cowboys faced many other dangers, too, like rattlesnakes, or having to pull a steer out of quicksand. As farmers and sheep ranchers fenced in more and more land, the cattle drives came to an end.

 FRUIT LEATHER

For hundreds of years, people throughout the world have preserved fruit by drying it in the sun. Native American tribes throughout North America followed this practice, and so did the pioneers in the West. Once the fruit was dried, the pioneers rolled it in oiled paper. Then, to use it for cooking, they peeled off some of the fruit, boiled it in water for a few minutes, and added it to their recipes. Many fruit-drying methods required several days of drying in the sun, but in this recipe, you'll be using a simpler technique that was brought to the frontier by pioneers from the southern United States.

INGREDIENTS

1 pound fresh apricots
½ pound peaches or pears, or a combination of the two
¼ cup sugar

EQUIPMENT

paper towels
paring knife
*blender or food processor (or a potato masher or heavy spoon and a
    mixing bowl)*
measuring cup
large bread board, cutting board, or countertop
rolling pin
airtight glass or plastic container
adult helper

MAKES

4 to 6 snack servings

1. Wash the fruit in cold running water and pat it dry with paper towels.

2. Ask your adult helper to use a paring knife to peel off the skins and cut the fruit into small pieces. Discard stems, pits, and seeds.

3. Place the fruits in a blender, food processor, or mixing bowl.

4. If you use a blender, have an adult help you pulse the fruit for about 15 seconds, 10 seconds longer for a food processor. If you're using a mixing bowl, mash and stir the fruit with a potato masher or the back of a heavy spoon. The fruit should look like jam or preserves.

5. Sprinkle the sugar on the board or countertop and spoon the fruit mixture onto the sugar.

The Chuck Wagon

A man named Charles Goodnight, one of the first ranchers to lead Texas longhorns on the long cattle drives, invented the chuck wagon. Goodnight's first chuck wagon was simply a kitchen cupboard nailed on the back of a ranch wagon. Before long, every ranch and cattle drive had copied Goodnight's invention. Ranchers and cowboys used the chuck wagon to carry blankets, saddles, ammunition, and medicine, as well as food. To prepare meals, the cook folded down the cabinet door to make a work counter. The chuck wagon also served as the cowboys' headquarters whenever they camped.

6. Use a rolling pin to roll the fruit flat, like a thin pancake, about ⅛ inch thick.

7. With a table knife, cut the fruit into strips, about 1 inch wide and 4 inches long.

8. Roll up each piece into a tight roll. Sample one or two pieces and store the rest in an airtight container. Your fruit leather will stay fresh at room temperature for 10 weeks or more.

RANCH VISITORS

While Tom was away on the cattle drive, a young pioneer family named Wilson came to visit the ranch. The Wilsons were starting a farm about fifty miles east of the Thayer ranch on the Great Plains—a vast area of prairie grasses that stretched from the Mississippi River to the Rocky Mountains. They wanted to buy two longhorn calves to add to their farm's livestock. The Wilson's daughter, Donna, was Amy's age and their two sons were just a little older than Tad. Amy was delighted to have a new friend to ride with, and Tad spent the days tagging along after the Wilson boys as they explored the whole ranch.

Donna told Amy about traveling west for ten weeks in a wagon train from Missouri.

They had chosen to come by covered wagon rather than the railroad so that they could bring their horses and farm equipment. Donna showed Amy how to make the cap she was wearing and how to make a pinwheel like one she had attached to their covered wagon. She also showed Amy the diary she had kept on the long, slow journey to the frontier.

 **PIONEER DIARY**

From the 1840s to the 1890s, wagon trains rumbled slowly westward from Missouri across the Great Plains. Some continued west through the Rocky Mountains to Oregon and California, a journey that could take six months or more. Many pioneer women kept diaries as they traveled. They wrote about hardships, including sickness and the scarcity of water, and about the dangers, which occasionally included attacks by Native American warriors. They also wrote about the beauty of the land, the adventure of starting a new life, and the close friendships that developed on the wagon trains. In this project, you'll make a diary much like the ones the pioneers made, although you won't have to bind the blank sheets of paper into the book as they did. Use your diary to record daily events, observations about the weather and seasons, or your own private thoughts.

MATERIALS

several sheets of newspaper
cotton print fabric, about 12-by-14 inches
small spiral notebook, about 6½-by-9 inches
pencil
ruler
scissors
craft glue or white glue

1 sheet construction paper in color to match fabric

1. Spread newspaper on your work surface. Place the fabric print side down on the newspaper.

2. Open the notebook and position it on the fabric. Trace a pencil line around the notebook onto the fabric.

3. Use ruler and pencil to draw another line around the notebook, 1 inch wider on each side and 2 inches higher at the top and bottom, as shown in the drawing.

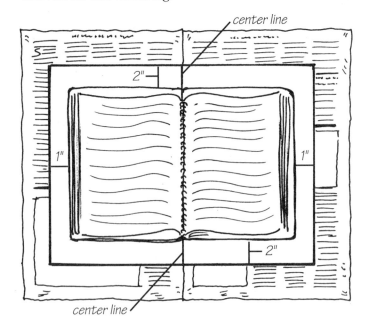

center line

2"

1"

1"

2"

center line

4. Cut out the fabric with scissors along the outside lines.

5. With ruler and pencil, draw a line down the center of the fabric from top to bottom (where the wire binding would be). Cut along that line to divide the fabric in half.

6. Place the two fabric pieces, print side down, on your work surface. Position the open notebook on top of the fabric, so that each cover of the notebook fits over the fabric, as shown.

7. Use pencil and ruler to draw cutting lines at each of the four corners, as indicated in the drawing by the broken lines. The cutting lines should just touch the corners of the notebook covers.

8. Cut away the fabric at each corner. This will create six cover flaps, each about 2 inches wide.

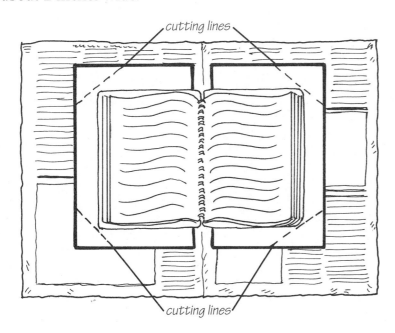

cutting lines

cutting lines

Homesteaders on the Great Plains

American pioneers began settling the Great Plains in the 1870s and 1880s. This huge expanse of tall grasses and few trees had once been called the Great American Desert because people thought the thick, matted grass—called sod—could not be plowed and that the climate was too harsh for farming. But new plows made of steel could cut through the sod, and new types of wheat could survive the bitterly cold winters.

To encourage settlers, the United States government passed the Homestead Act of 1862, granting 160 acres to anyone who would settle on the prairie. The thousands of settlers who took advantage of the new law were called "homesteaders." Since there were few trees, the homesteaders cut blocks of sod to build their first houses. These hardy pioneers faced a difficult life at first, but soon their fields of wheat and corn covered the Great Plains.

9. Move all of the notebook pages to one side so that you can see the inside of the cover on the opposite side.

10. Make sure the notebook is centered on the fabric. Spread glue on the three cover flaps, fold over the flaps, and press them in place against the inside of the cover.

11. Repeat step 10 for the other cover.

12. Close the book and glue the loose edge of fabric to the outside cover next to the spiral binding.

13. With ruler and pencil, measure two pieces of construction paper about 5 inches wide and 8 inches high. Cut out the two pieces.

14. Glue one piece of construction paper to the inside of each cover. This will keep the fabric from fraying and it will hide any glue that shows through the fabric. Your pioneer diary is now ready to record your thoughts and observations.

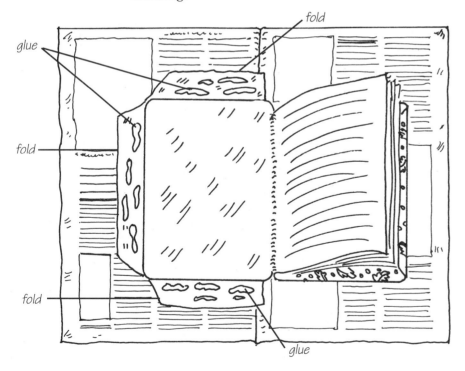

 **PINWHEEL**

A pinwheel works like a miniature windmill—a device with long wing-like blades that turn in the wind. Windmill power has been used for more than one thousand years to raise water from wells and to turn wheels for grinding grain into flour or meal. Many homesteading families used wind-mills to lift water from wells that had to be dug deep into the dry prairie soil.

Pinwheels were one of the most popular toys of the 1800s. Children could buy cardboard pin-wheels at circuses and fairs, but many preferred to make their own out of stiff paper, much the way you'll be doing in this project.

MATERIALS

1 sheet of stiff paper or construction paper (a manila file folder works well)
ruler
pencil
crayon or marking pen, any color
scissors
straight pin
long pencil with eraser

1. Place the sheet of paper on your work surface. Use ruler and pencil to draw a 6-inch square. Cut out the square.

2. With ruler and pencil, draw diagonal lines (from corner to opposite corner) on the square, but stop the lines about 1 inch from the center, as indicated by the broken lines in the drawing.

3. With the crayon or marking pen, decorate the four corners with stars. Notice the positioning of the stars in the drawing. (The positioning will help you with the folding in step 6.)

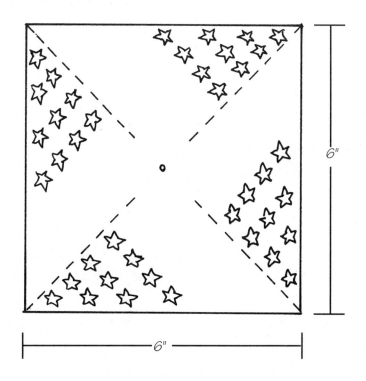

4. With scissors, cut along the four diagonal lines toward the center of the square. Remember to stop cutting about 1 inch from the center.

5. If you wish, you can turn the square over and decorate the other side.

6. With the starred side facing away from you, bend each of the four corners over, so that the four points meet at the center. Overlap the points a little so that the pin can go through all four.

7. Push the pin through all four corners and through the center point. Leave the head of the pin sticking out a little from the pinwheel so that it will turn freely.

8. Press the pin into the side of the pencil eraser. Your pinwheel is complete. You can make it spin by blowing on it, running with it, or simply holding it to the wind.

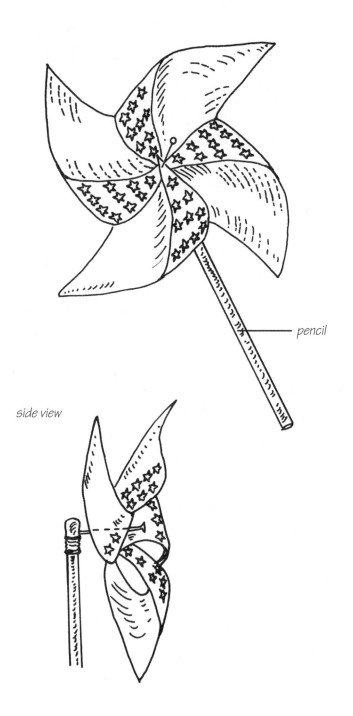

pencil

side view

PROJECT PIONEER CAP

On the wagon trains going west, girls made simple bonnets and caps, mostly to keep the dust and dirt out of their hair. They usually put long ribbons on these hats so they could tie them under their chins during stormy or windy weather. Here is an easy-to-make cap that was popular from the 1700s to about 1900.

MATERIALS

piece of white cotton or linen fabric, at least
   18 inches square
2 pencils
ruler
12-inch piece of string
scissors
narrow satin ribbon, about ½ inch wide and 48 inches
   long, any color
helper (optional)

1. To draw a circle on the cloth, lay the fabric flat on your work surface, then tie two pencils together with string. Use a ruler to measure the string so that it stretches exactly 9 inches from one pencil to the other.

2. Hold one pencil firmly, point down, in the middle of the fabric. You might find it easier to have a helper hold the pencil in position.

3. Hold the second pencil, stretching the string out the full 9 inches. You've now made a drawing compass for a circle that will have a 9-inch radius and a diameter of 18 inches.

4. While holding the first pencil in place, and keeping the string straight, move the outer pencil all the way around the inner one, marking the cloth as you go. When you get back to your starting point, you should have a perfect circle.

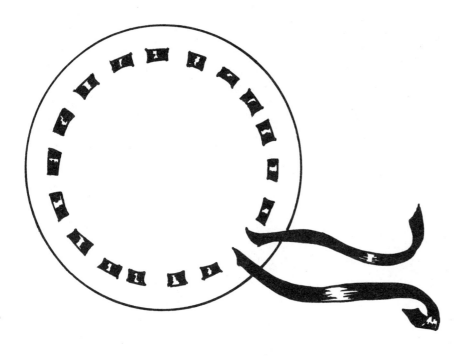

5. Cut out the circle with scissors.

6. With pencil and ruler, make short pencil marks all the way around the outer part of the circle, about 1½ inches from the edge of the cloth. Space the marks about 1 inch apart.

7. With scissors, cut a narrow slit at each pencil mark. The slits should be just wide enough for the ribbon to fit through.

8. Run the ribbon in and out of the slits, as shown in the drawing.

9. Place the cap on your head, positioning it toward the back of your head. Slowly pull the ribbon ends and use your hands to adjust the puckers as the cap tightens to the shape of your head.

10. Tie the ribbon ends in a bow, just tight enough for the cap to fit comfortably. Your pioneer cap is ready to wear.

A TRIP TO CHEYENNE

In mid-July, Tom and Kip returned to the ranch from the cattle drive. Although he was saddle-weary and eager to sleep in his own bed again, Tom enjoyed telling the family about his adventures on the trail.

A few days after Tom's return, the Thayers rode the ranch wagon into Cheyenne, the fast-growing town that was the capital of Wyoming Territory. The town had been started only eleven years earlier, in 1867, when the building of the transcontinental railroad reached that point and a station was established. By 1878, Cheyenne was a major shipping point for cattle ranchers. The town was also a supply center for farm families settling on the prairie and for miners heading for the gold fields of Dakota Territory.

Amy and Tom loved the noise and bustle of the dusty streets, which were clogged with delivery wagons, carriages, horses, and cov-ered wagons. All around them they heard the buzz of saws and clang of hammers as work crews constructed new buildings. Tad led everyone into a shop owned by a family of Chinese immigrants and Pa bought a bag of almond cookies.

Late in the afternoon, they visited a traveling circus on the outskirts of town. While Tad was fascinated by a dancing bear, Amy and Tom were thrilled by the acrobats. Back at the ranch, Ma Thayer helped the children make circus cutouts, and Pa showed them how to make a toy balancing acrobat.

PROJECT BALANCING ACROBAT

Children—and grownups—in the 1800s were fond of all kinds of balancing toys. The earliest examples were made of wood, but in the late 1800s, metal balancing toys became more popular, usually with wires attached to weights to create the balance. In this project, you'll make a wood and cardboard version of one of the most popular toys, an acrobatic dancer who balanced on one foot.

MATERIALS

1 piece of thin cardboard or white poster board, about 6 inches square

pencil

ruler

scissors

crayons or colored pencils

thin dowels, garden stakes, or chopsticks, at least 15 inches long

coping saw or craft knife (to be used by an adult helper)

large nail

large cork (available in most supermarkets and discount department stores)

white glue

strong thread, black or white, 36 inches long

adult helper

1. Place the cardboard flat on your work surface. Copy the drawing of the acrobat and her base on the cardboard with pencil. The figure and the base should be about 4½ inches high.

2. Cut out the figure and base with scissors.

3. Use crayons or colored pencils to color the acrobat and the base above the fold line. Use any colors you wish. Set the figure aside.

4. Ask your adult helper to cut the dowel or other material into two lengths of 6½ inches and one of 1½ inches. The adult can also use a coping saw or craft knife to cut a small notch in one end of the short dowel, as shown in the picture.

5. To attach the dowels to the cork, have the adult help you make a nail hole in the bottom of the cork. Place the hole exactly in the center. Make two holes opposite each other in the lower part of the cork, as shown in the drawing.

6. Spread a little glue on the uncut tip of the short dowel and work it into the hole in the bottom of the cork. Make sure the notch in the dowel extends straight from front to back.

fold line

4½"

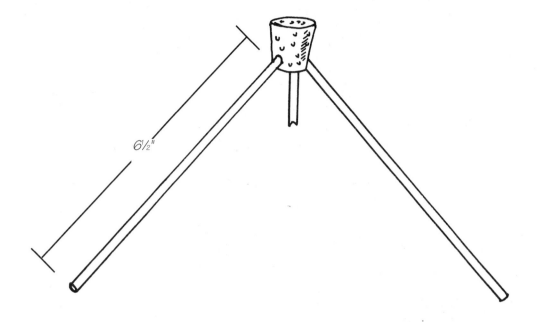

6½"

7. Insert the long dowels into the sides the same way. These dowels should be angled away from the cork, as in the drawing. Allow the glue to dry for 10 to 15 minutes.

8. Fold back the base of the acrobat along the fold line so she will stand upright. Spread glue on the bottom of the base and attach the acrobat firmly to the top of the cork. Let the glue dry for a few minutes.

Wild West Towns

The cattle towns and mining settlements of the West grew so fast that the people called them "boom towns." Since there wasn't time to form a local government, the towns often began as untamed places, where powerful outlaws ruled, while gambling dens and saloons multiplied. Even after law and order were established, and a sheriff or marshal had been hired to enforce the law, disturbances were frequent. After a long, hard trail ride, for example, cowboys often let off steam by firing their revolvers in the air or annoying people on the street. They sometimes drove their herds right down the main street, forcing people to scramble for safety.

As wild as the boom towns were, they were never as wild as people in the East imagined. Stories made it seem that gunfights and hangings took place almost every day. The truth was that most frontier people, including cowboys, were law-abiding citizens who never even saw a shootout. Even famous lawmen like Bat Masterson and Wild Bill Hickock rarely had to draw their guns.

9. Place the balancing acrobat on the tip of your index finger, as indicated in the picture. With a little practice, you'll find that she easily keeps her balance.

10. Tie one end of the thread to the back of a chair, a doorknob, or a cabinet handle. Stretch the thread out straight with one hand and, with the other hand, fit the notch in the short dowel over the thread. After a few tries, you'll be able to balance the acrobat on the thread.

11. For an extra challenge, try holding the stretched thread a little lower. The acrobat will slide down the thread toward your hand.

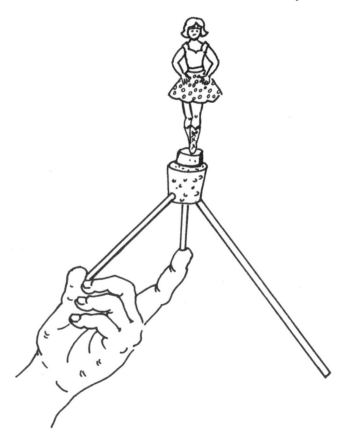

PROJECT CIRCUS CUTOUTS

Ever since paper was invented in China nearly 2,000 years ago, people throughout the world have been fascinated by the thousands of shapes that can be created by folding and cutting pieces of paper. Paper snowflakes are one popular form of cutout art. By making several different folds, you can also create a wide variety of connected shapes, including people. In this project, you'll use four simple folds to make a group of circus acrobats. On your own, you can experiment with other folds and figures and see what happens.

You'll need a long, narrow piece of thin paper for your circus cutouts. You can use wrapping paper, rolled paper like the paper used in fax machines and calculators, or, if necessary, overlap two sheets of typing paper and glue them together.

MATERIALS
long, narrow piece of paper, about 4 inches wide and
    14 inches long
ruler
pencil
scissors
black felt-tip pen
crayons or colored pencils

1. Place the piece of paper on your work surface, with the long way stretching from left to right.

2. Fold the paper in half the long way, with the fold on the left.

3. Fold it in half again the same way. The two open ends should be on the right.

4. Now fold it in half from top to bottom, bringing the edges farthest away from you down over the other half. Your book-like folded paper should now measure about 2 inches by 3½ inches.

5. Position the folded sheets on your work surface so that the longest fold is on the right.

6. Draw one half of an acrobat figure against the fold, as shown in the picture. Make sure that the body and head reach all the way to the fold. The acrobat's foot should touch the bottom edge and the arm should end exactly at the top fold. Notice that the end of the arm is lined up directly above the foot.

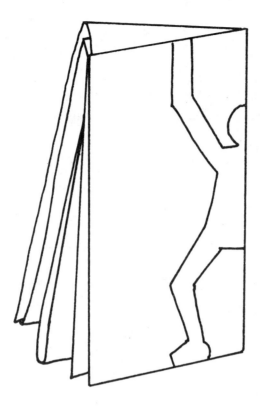

7. Carefully cut out the figure. Be certain that the scissors cut through all eight layers of paper.

8. Gently unfold the paper. You should have four acrobats balanced on top of each other.

9. Use the felt-tip pen to draw hair, eyes, nose, mouth, and any other details you wish. Give each acrobat a different look.

10. Design and color outfits for each of the figures.

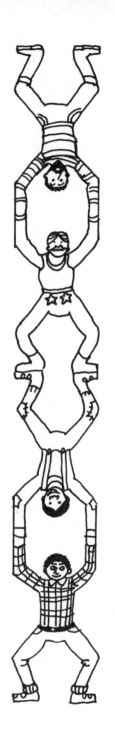

CHINESE ALMOND COOKIES

Each region of China has its own special style of cooking. When Chinese immigrants began arriving in the United States in the mid-1800s, they brought with them many of the delicious recipes from their homeland. Some of the immigrants established restaurants and bakeries. Chinese food soon became popular throughout the country. In traditional Chinese cooking, the main meal of the day would usually include fruit for dessert. Sweets, like the tasty cookies you'll make in this recipe, were usually served with afternoon tea.

INGREDIENTS

¼ pound butter or vegetable shortening, softened
¾ cup sugar
1 egg
½ teaspoon vanilla
1 tablespoon whole milk or light cream
1¼ cups all-purpose flour
dash of salt (about ⅛ teaspoon)
¼ teaspoon baking powder
¾ teaspoon almond extract (available in the spice section of supermarkets)
36 blanched almond halves or 18 whole almonds cut in half

EQUIPMENT

measuring cup
measuring spoons
2 medium-size mixing bowls
wooden mixing spoon
eggbeater
2 cookie sheets
paring knife (to be used by an adult for cutting whole almonds)
teaspoon
adult helper

MAKES

about 3 dozen cookies

1. Preheat the oven to 350°F.

2. Place the softened butter in a mixing bowl and stir it well with a mixing spoon to make it creamy. If you use vegetable shortening, you won't need to stir it much.

3. Add the sugar to the butter or shortening, a little at a time. As you add the sugar, stir constantly. Keep stirring until the mixture lightens in color.

Chinese Immigrants on the Frontier

Immigrants from China played an important part in the settling of the West. The first Chinese came to California after gold was discovered in 1848. By 1870, 50,000 of the Asian newcomers had settled in California, while thousands more moved to other states. More than 9,000 Chinese workers helped build the transcontinental railroad. They became famous for their daring and skill in carving passageways for the tracks through the rugged Sierra Nevada and Rocky Mountains. By the late 1870s, many had settled in Colorado, Wyoming, and the Dakota Territory.

4. Add the egg, vanilla, and milk or cream. Beat the mixture well with an eggbeater until all the ingredients are blended.

5. Place the flour, salt, and baking powder in the other mixing bowl. Stir the mixture with a clean, dry spoon.

6. Add the flour mixture to the first mixture, a little at a time, stirring constantly.

7. Add the almond extract and mix the ingredients well with the eggbeater.

8. Using one slightly rounded teaspoon for each cookie, place the dough on ungreased cookie sheets. Flatten each cookie a little with the spoon and allow about an inch of space between them.

9. Press a half almond onto the center of each cookie. If you use whole almonds, ask your adult helper to cut them in half the long way with a paring knife.

10. With the adult's help, bake the cookies for 8 to 10 minutes. Check the cookies frequently. They're done when they turn golden brown.

CHAPTER THREE

Autumn

In autumn, the Thayers held the second roundup of the year. The purpose of this roundup was to choose the cattle they planned to sell. Just as farmers harvested their crops in the autumn, ranchers harvested their herds. The sales provided them with the income they needed to keep their ranches going.

For more than two weeks, Pa and the cowboys rounded up the steers, which had become widely scattered over the open range. They then separated, or cut out, 300 steers to drive to the railroad depot in Cheyenne for shipment to a meat-packing company in Chicago. Tom felt very grown up working as the wrangler, and Amy also had an important job. She kept a count, or tally, of the steers the cowboys separated from the main herd. Since the men worked in pairs, bringing cattle from different directions, Amy found it wasn't easy to keep an accurate tally.

A JOURNEY TO FORT LARAMIE

After Pa and the cowboys returned from Cheyenne, they cut out a smaller herd of sixty steers to drive to Fort Laramie. The fort, about 80 miles north of Cheyenne, was on one of the main trails the earlier pioneers had used to travel to Oregon and California. Army troops stationed at the fort had protected the wagon trains. Pa had made arrangements to sell the longhorns to the army and distribute some to the Sioux who traded at the fort.

The fort commander had assured Pa that the entire Thayer family could safely make the trip to Fort Laramie, so the family rode in the ranch wagon ahead of the cattle drive, giving Amy, Tom, and Tad a week to visit the fort. They enjoyed watching the soldiers drill and work with their horses, and they wandered around the twenty buildings that made up the fort.

A number of Sioux families were camped outside the fort and came in often to trade. Outside the fort's

trading post, Ma Thayer, Amy, and Tom watched Sioux women weaving baskets. Tom admired a Cheyenne war shield on display in the post, and Amy liked the designs on an owner stick. Pa said he would help them make these things when they were back on the ranch.

PROJECT OWNER STICK

When Native American families gathered firewood or wild foods, they marked the pile they had collected with an owner stick, or possession marker. The markings on the stick identified the family. This way, no one else would touch their collection and they could return for it later. In a similar way, hunters marked their game by sticking an arrow in the ground that had the hunter's markings. Use your owner stick to mark your possessions or just to decorate your room.

MATERIALS

½-inch dowel, about 24 inches long
¼-inch dowel, about 18 inches long
¼-inch dowel, about 12 inches long
ruler
pencil
coping saw (to be used by an adult)
white glue
twine, about 36 inches
scissors
marking pens or felt-tip pens (blue, black, red, yellow)
scraps of yarn or narrow ribbon (any color)
3 or more feathers, real or made from paper (feathers are available in the craft and hobby section of most discount department stores)
scraps of white paper, if needed for making feathers
string, about 8 inches
adult helper

1. If the dowels need to be cut to the right lengths, ask an adult to help you use the coping saw.

2. Have the adult help you use the coping saw to cut a notch in the ½-inch dowel, about 6 inches from the top, and a second notch about 6 inches below the first notch. The notches should be just wide enough for the ¼-inch dowels to fit snugly. Don't cut the notches very deep (⅛ inch is enough).

3. Place a drop of glue in the upper notch and press the 18-inch dowel against it. Make sure the dowel is centered.

4. Without waiting for the glue to dry, tie a piece of twine around the thicker dowel, then wrap it around the thinner dowel two or three times in a criss-cross, as shown in the picture. Cut the twine and tie the ends in a firm double knot.

5. Repeat steps 3 and 4 to attach the 12-inch crosspiece to the lower notch.

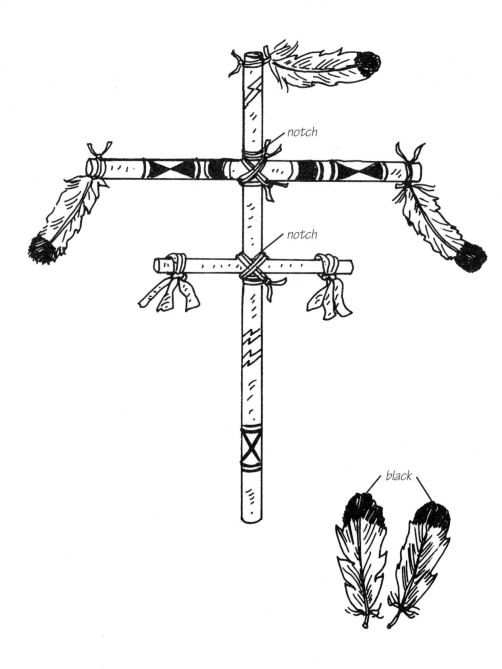

notch

notch

black

6. Use marking pens to draw designs on all three pieces. Copy the decorations shown or create your own, using any combination of the four colors. In the picture, the upright dowel has a lightning symbol near the top, and two more farther down—this was a favorite symbol of many tribes.

7. Tie scraps of yarn or ribbon around the ends of one of the crosspieces.

8. Use string to attach feathers in other places, as suggested in the picture. To make paper feathers, simply copy the design shown on scraps of white paper, cut them out, and add black markings. Your owner stick is now ready to use.

PROJECT — CHEYENNE SHIELD

Warriors of the Great Plains tribes placed great importance on their war shields. They made the shields out of the toughest part of the buffalo hide, allowing the hide to shrink over a smoky fire. These small shields, which were only about 18 inches across, were strong enough to stop an arrow, and they could even slow down the speed of a bullet.

The shield was even more important for its "medicine," or spirit power, which warriors believed would protect them in battle. They painted designs on the shield that they hoped would add to that power. The copy of a Cheyenne shield that you'll make in this project has a blue eagle for protection. The lightning symbol at the bottom shows the great power of the shield, and the red fringe extends the magic throughout the day, since red is the color for day.

Warriors hung their shields at the back of the tepee and, in good weather, hung them on a tripod in front of the tepee. You can hang your shield on the wall, or make a simple tripod by tying three sticks or dowels together.

MATERIALS

several sheets of newspaper
strong, flexible wire, like a wreath frame (a metal coat hanger will work)
pliers
ruler
adhesive tape
scissors
drawing compass
chamois at least 16 inches square (available in the automotive section of
*   most supermarkets and discount department stores)*
hole punch

The Buffalo Hunters

The people of the Plains tribes—the Sioux, Cheyenne, Kiowa, and many others—depended on the huge herds of buffalo that roamed the Great Plains. The buffalo provided meat to cook or to dry into pemmican. The Native Americans used the buffalo hide to make clothing, blankets, moccasins, tepees, and other items. They fashioned bones into tools, weapons, utensils, and ornaments. And they used the tendons that connected muscles to make strings for their bows.

The people of each tribe followed a herd as it migrated north or south across the prairie. The hunters were expert horsemen and crack shots either with bows and arrows or with rifles. The women did most of the work of skinning the animal, preparing the meat, and curing the hide.

rawhide lacing (sold as shoelaces), or twine
pencil
acrylic paints: white (optional), blue, red, yellow,
  green, black
small paintbrush
scrap of red felt, cotton, or ribbon
white glue or transparent tape
2 or 3 small feathers, real or made from scraps of
  white paper (feathers are available in the craft and
  hobby section of most discount department stores)
adult helper

1. Spread several sheets of newspaper over your work surface.

2. Make a circle of wire about 10 inches in diameter (across). If you use a metal coat hanger, ask an adult to use pliers to bend the wire into the circle. Whatever kind of wire you use, overlap the ends several inches and wind adhesive tape around the overlap several times to hold the circle firmly.

3. Spread the chamois flat. Use the drawing compass to measure and draw a circle about 15 inches in diameter. Cut out the circle with scissors.

4. With the hole punch, make ten holes in the chamois about ½ inch in from the edge. Space the holes evenly in five pairs directly across from each other. (Lay the ruler across the center of the fabric and punch a hole at either end of the ruler.)

5. Place the wire frame on top of the chamois, center it, and fold the edges of the chamois over the wire, as shown.

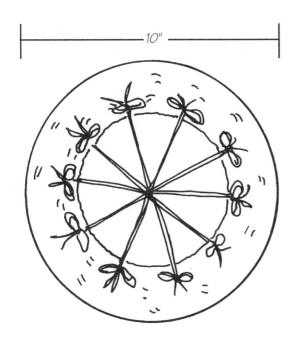

_10"_

6. Run a piece of rawhide lacing or twine through one of the holes and tie it to the edge of the chamois in a double knot. Stretch the lacing across to the opposite hole. Run it through the hole, pull it fairly tight, and tie another knot.

7. Repeat step 6 to connect the other four pairs of holes with lacing or twine. Turn the shield over. If the chamois fits too loosely, tighten some of the lacings; if it fits too tightly and puckers in some places, try loosening one or two knots. Cut off the extra lacing.

8. On the front of the shield, copy the design shown in the picture, drawing lightly with pencil.

9. If you want a white background, paint the entire shield white. Allow the paint to dry, then paint the eagle blue and the lightning yellow. Use the colors listed for the four stars.

10. With scissors, cut a narrow band of red felt, cotton, or ribbon, about 16 inches long.

11. Attach the red trim with glue or transparent tape across the top of the shield and let it hang down one side.

12. Use glue or transparent tape to attach two or three feathers at the bottom of the red trim, as shown in the picture. (To make paper feathers, see the Owner Stick project.) Your Cheyenne war shield is finished.

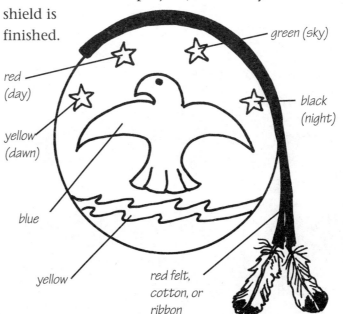

red (day)

green (sky)

yellow (dawn)

black (night)

blue

yellow

red felt, cotton, or ribbon

The End of the Buffalo Herds

Until the mid-1800s, about 20 million buffalo roamed the Great Plains from Canada to Texas. The herds were so enormous that they made the earth shake as they thundered across the prairie. It could take four or five hours for a herd to pass a given point.

As more and more Americans moved into the West, they killed the buffalo in ever-growing numbers. Some hunted the animals to sell the hides to be made into buffalo robes, in factories in the East. Others found they could make money by selling buffalo meat to railroad companies to feed the thousands of workers. And, as the railroads moved West, the trains stopped to let passengers shoot the animals for sport, leaving the carcasses to rot.

By the 1880s, the great herds were gone and the buffalo was close to extinction. The American people finally realized that this slaughter had been a terrible waste. Conservation efforts saved the buffalo from extinction, and today more than 10,000 of these majestic animals are protected by the government.

 **WOVEN BASKET**

Most Native American women were skilled basket makers. Baskets were made in many different shapes and sizes. Some were used for gathering and storing food, others for cooking. Baskets were also used as cradles and as fish traps.

Every tribe had its favorite material for basket making. Many tribes used grasses or reeds; others preferred slender willow branches or long, thin strips of wood, called splints. Some women could even weave beautiful baskets out of pine needles, porcupine quills, or horse hair. In this project, you'll make your basket out of lightweight poster board and decorate it with symbols used by Sioux basket weavers.

MATERIALS
1 sheet of lightweight poster board, tan or light brown, at least
 12-by-24 inches
ruler or yardstick
pencil
scissors
stapler
white glue
4 to 6 paper clips
marking pens or felt-tip pens: blue, yellow, red

1. On the poster board, use ruler or yardstick and pencil to mark a strip 1 inch wide and 24 inches long. Cut out the strip with scissors.

2. Repeat step 1 to make a total of 12 strips. You can use the first strip to make the pencil mark for the other strips.

3. Place 4 strips on your work surface side by side. Weave 4 other strips over and under the first 4, as shown in the drawing.

4. Push the strips together so there is no space between them, creating a tight weave.

5. Put a staple in each of the four corners of the woven part. This completes the bottom of your basket.

6. Fold all the unwoven ends up to start the sides, as indicated in the picture.

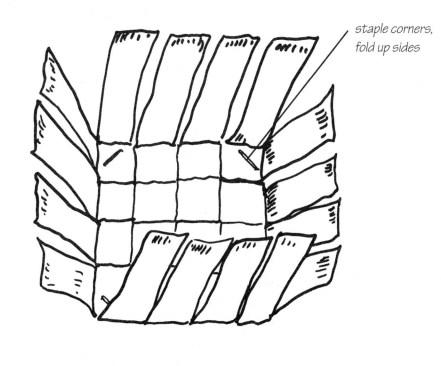

staple corners, fold up sides

7. Weave the remaining 4 strips in and out of the side strips. Overlap the ends and secure them with a little glue. You can slide a paper clip over the ends to hold the overlap in place until the glue dries; then remove the paper clips.

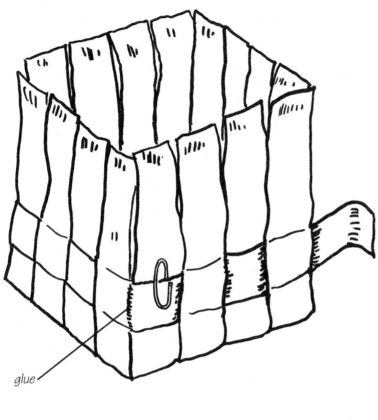

glue

8. When all 4 side strips have been woven in place, bend the upright ends inside the basket and glue them in place.

9. Use marking pens to decorate the sides of the basket with symbols. Four common Sioux symbols are shown, or you can design your own, or find a library book of Native American symbols.

fold over and glue

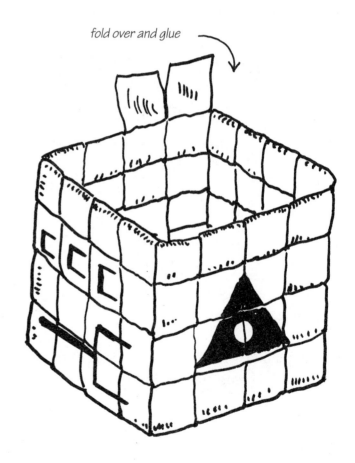

the trail parts

horse tracks

dragonfly

tipi

lightning

ROUNDUP CELEBRATION

When the Thayers returned from Fort Laramie, they held a party to celebrate the roundup and a successful ranching year. They invited neighboring ranch families and friends from Cheyenne. Miguel was in charge of the cooking, with help from four other ranch cooks. Amy and her mother baked stacks of sourdough bread and biscuits. Tom helped Pa and the cowboys create makeshift tables and benches by placing boards across wooden barrels. They also made a wooden platform for dancing, the favorite form of entertainment on the frontier.

Nearly a hundred people came to the celebration, which began before noon and lasted far into the night. Some of the cowboys provided music for dancing and singing with guitars, banjos, and a violin. The children played Indian games like toss and catch and basket toss, then joined the grown-ups at the

tables piled with food. They ate steaks, roast beef, squash, beans and baked beans, and bread, with cake, pie, apples, and dried fruit for dessert. Amy and Tom especially like the Plains Indian dessert called *wo-jopee* and Miguel's specialty, *frijoles refritos*.

PROJECT FRIJOLES REFRITOS

Frijoles refritos (free-HOLE-ees ray-FREE-tohs) is a Mexican dish; in English the name means "refried beans." *Frijoles refritos* is one of many dishes that trace their origins to Mexico and the Mexican settlers who lived in what is now the Southwest of the United States. Other foods that come to us from this Mexican heritage are tacos, tortillas, enchiladas, burritos, and many others.

Beans of all kinds were popular on the western frontier because they could be stored for a long time and were packed with flavor and nutrition. But, as you'll see, some kinds of beans take a long time to prepare. For this reason, many ranch cooks did not take them in the chuck wagon on cattle drives or roundups. Other cooks insisted on using them for cooking on the trail. They said that dishes like *frijoles refritos* were worth the time. Try this recipe and you are likely to agree.

INGREDIENTS
1 pound (2 cups) dried pinto beans
½ pound bacon or salt pork, diced (cut into small pieces)
1 clove garlic, minced (cut into tiny pieces)
1 small onion, diced (about 1/2 cup)
½ teaspoon salt
½ cup cooking oil
½ cup diced or shredded Monterey Jack or mild

cheddar cheese
salt and pepper to taste

EQUIPMENT
measuring cups
measuring spoons
1 large saucepan (2 to 4 quarts), with cover
paring knife or food chopper (to be used by an adult)
cutting board
colander or large kitchen strainer
large skillet
mixing spoon
fork
serving bowl
adult helper

MAKES
4 to 6 servings

1. Place the beans in the colander and rinse under running water. Then put them in the saucepan.

2. Fill the saucepan with enough water to cover the beans. Ask your adult helper to bring the beans to a boil and continue boiling for about 3 minutes.

3. Turn off the heat. Cover the saucepan and let the beans soak for one hour.

4. While the pinto beans are soaking, ask your adult helper to use a paring knife or food chopper to cut the bacon or salt pork, mince the garlic, and dice the onion.

5. Drain the beans in the colander, then put them back in the saucepan. Add the bacon, garlic, and onion.

6. Fill the saucepan with water so that the beans are covered. Ask your adult helper to bring the mixture to a boil and then turn the heat down to simmer. Simmer, without stirring, until the beans are very soft. This will take about 3 hours. Add more water when necessary to keep the beans moist

7. When the beans are soft, turn off the heat. Sprinkle the salt over them, then drain off the remaining water.

8. Have your adult helper heat the cooking oil in a large skillet.

9. With the heat on low, ask the adult to help you use a mixing spoon to place a spoonful of beans in the oil. Mash the beans with the back of

a fork, or with the mixing spoon, until the beans and oil are blended.

10. Continue adding oil and beans, mashing them together, until all the beans are in the skillet.

11. Fry the beans a few minutes longer, so that they are a little crisp at the edges of the pan, smooth and creamy in the middle.

12. Turn off the heat, spoon the beans into a serving bowl, and stir in the cheese. Serve warm. Each person can add salt and pepper to taste.

The Hispanic Heritage of the Southwest

In the 1500s, the European nation of Spain established a sprawling colonial empire in what Europeans called the New World (North and South America). This empire covered much of South America, all of present-day Mexico, and what is now the Southwest of the United States. The Spanish, or Hispanic, influence on this entire region has been long lasting. The Spanish brought their language, their Catholic religion, their styles of cooking, and their arts and crafts to the New World. Some of the Spanish people mixed with the Native American population, and some with people brought from Africa as slaves. Most of the people of modern Mexico and much of South America are descendants of this blending of peoples.

The people and culture of the Southwest continue to reflect the Hispanic influence. Even place names, like San Antonio, Santa Fe, and Las Vegas, are reminders of American Hispanic heritage.

WO-JOPEE—SIOUX BLACKBERRY DESSERT

Ranch families and settlers on the northern Great Plains learned to make a wonderful blackberry dish from the people of the Sioux tribes. The Sioux called the dessert *wo-jopee*. They made it from fresh or dried wild blackberries and sweetened it with wild honey. Settlers and ranchers changed the recipe a little, using sugar as a sweetener, with a touch of lemon juice. You'll find that this more modern version of *wo-jopee* is delicious and refreshing.

INGREDIENTS

about 14 ounces blackberries, fresh, frozen, or canned
1½ cups sugar
1½ cups water (2 cups if you're using fresh berries)
4 tablespoons all-purpose flour
1 teaspoon lemon juice
whipped cream or ice cream (optional)

EQUIPMENT

measuring cups
measuring spoons
2-quart saucepan
colander or large kitchen strainer
mixing bowl
wire whisk
mixing spoon
adult helper

MAKES

about 4 servings

1. If you're using frozen blackberries, place them in a saucepan and let them thaw at room temperature (30 minutes to 1 hour). If you're using fresh blackberries, add ½ cup of water and ask your adult helper to simmer them for about 10 minutes.

2. Drain the juice into a mixing bowl by pouring the berries through a colander or strainer. Save the juice in the bowl.

3. Put the blackberries back in the saucepan and gently stir in the sugar.

4. Add the water to the blackberry juice in the mixing bowl.

5. Stir the flour into the juice a little at a time, stirring constantly with the wire whisk to prevent lumps. Continue stirring until the flour is completely mixed in.

6. Pour the juice mixture into the saucepan with the berries and sugar.

7. Ask your adult helper to bring the mixture slowly to a boil. Stir frequently as the mixture heats.

8. Reduce the heat to simmer and let the mixture simmer for 10 to 12 minutes, with frequent stirring

9. Turn off the heat and stir in the lemon juice.

10. Allow the mixture to cool, then chill it in the refrigerator for an hour. Serve the *wo-jopee* cold by itself, or topped with a little whipped cream, or use it as a topping for ice cream.

PROJECT THE GAME OF TOSS AND CATCH

Many Native American tribes played some version of this game. Some tribes used a piece of bone for the target, while others used a stiff piece of rawhide, or even the shell of a gourd or pumpkin. The early colonists had brought a similar game called cup and ball, from Europe. In the European game, the player tossed a ball in the air and tried to catch it in a small cup that was attached to the ball with string.

Instead of bone, rawhide, or pumpkin shell, you can make your game of toss and catch with cardboard. By stapling two pieces of cardboard together, your target will have as much weight as the Native American targets. In all its versions, this is a good game for developing hand-eye coordination (having the eye and hand work together).

MATERIALS

scrap of poster board or cardboard, about 6 inches
  square
ruler
pencil
scissors
hole punch
stapler
thin dowel, stick, pencil, or chopstick, 8 to 10 inches
  long

24-inch piece of string
2 players (or 2 teams)

1. On the poster board or cardboard, measure and draw a triangle with each side 3 inches long. Cut out the triangle with scissors. Round off the corners a little.

2. Use this triangle as a pattern to make a second triangle exactly the same size.

3. With the hole punch, make one small hole in the corner of one triangle. Make four larger holes, as shown in the drawing, by using the punch several times to enlarge each hole. These four holes should be large enough for the dowel or stick to pass through easily. Make the center hole slightly larger than the others so that one hole is easier to score in than the others.

4. Place this triangle over the triangle without holes. Staple the two triangles together with about four staples along each of the three sides.

5. Use the hole punch to make exactly the same holes in the second triangle, so that the holes go all the way through both triangles.

6. Tie one end of the string through the small hole in your triangle target piece. Tie the other end to the dowel or stick, about in the middle. Tie a tight double knot.

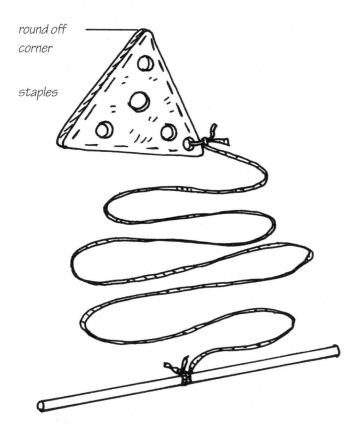

round off corner

staples

7. To play, hold the stick in one hand. Toss the target in the air with the other hand and try to catch it on the stick by having the stick go through one of the holes.

Scoring: Each player (or team) takes three turns or tosses. Score 1 point for each catch no matter which hole the stick goes through. Continue until one side scores 10 points.

For an extra challenge: Hold the stick in your hand and let the target hang toward the ground. Swing your arm and the hand holding the stick to toss the target in the air and catch it on the stick. In this version, a player cannot use the other hand.

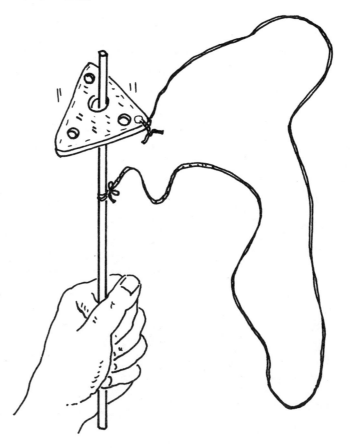

THE BRONCO BUSTER

A few days after the roundup celebration, the Thayer children started school. Amy and Tom rode their horses the four miles to the school, with Tad sitting on the back of Tom's saddle. The school was a simple one-room building, with an iron wood-stove in the middle. The 24 pupils sat on hard wooden benches while the young teacher, Miss Appleby, gave lessons in history, geography, math, reading, and penmanship. Because the children ranged in age from six to sixteen, she did her best to help the older children with more challenging lessons.

Tad was excited to be at school, but for the first two weeks Amy and Tom were impatient to get back to the ranch. Pa had hired a bronco buster to break in, or tame, some wild horses the cowboys had caught on the open range. The bronco buster, named Jake Drummond, charged five dollars for each horse. Amy, Tom,

and the cowboys were fascinated by the slow, gentle way he worked the horses. When the broncos bucked, they often threw him to the ground, but he was up on his feet in an instant and right back on the horse. By the time his work was finished, the ranch had nine new horses ready to ride. When he took time off, Jake showed the children how to tie different knots and how to make lariats from long pieces of rawhide.

PROJECT MAKING A LARIAT

Ropes, or lariats, were expensive to buy because they were made by skilled rope makers in a shop called a "ropewalk." To save money, many cowboys made their own lariats out of strips of rawhide or the twine-like material that came from the hemp plant. They tied shorter strands together to make longer pieces. To make a lariat 40 feet long, a cowboy needed about 120 feet of rawhide or hemp. He then took good care of his lariat by rubbing it with oil so that it would last a long time.

For your lariat, you'll use yarn instead of rawhide, twisting the strands the same way the cowboys did. You can use one long piece of yarn or, to vary the color, you can tie together shorter strands of different colors. Use your finished lariat to practice the knots in the next activity. After that, you can wear it as a belt, cutting it to a shorter length if necessary.

MATERIALS

yardstick or tape measure
about 24 feet of yarn, any color, or 4 6-foot lengths in
    different colors
scissors
2 pencils or scraps of dowel
helper

1. If you're using different colors of yarn, tie the shorter strands together into one long strand.

2. Fold the yarn in half. Insert a pencil or dowel through the loop made in the fold. Tie the other two ends around a second pencil or dowel.

3. With your helper holding one pencil or dowel and you the other, stand facing each other. Stretch the yarn out straight between you.

4. Start winding the yarn by twirling your pencil in one direction, while your helper twirls in the opposite direction. Keep the yarn between you taut, or pulled tightly, at all times. If you let it sag, the yarn will start to kink.

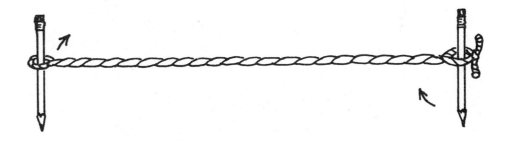

5. As you wind the yarn, the lariat will become shorter. You and your helper will start moving toward each other, but remember to keep the lariat taut.

6. When the strands are tightly twisted, hold the lariat firmly at the loop and remove the pencil or dowel. Your helper can do the same, holding the tied ends.

7. Still holding the loop firmly with one hand, reach toward your helper and grasp the middle of the lariat with your other hand. Continue to keep the rope taut and bring your loop end over to the helper's tied ends. This will double the thickness of the lariat.

8. You will feel the four strands start twisting together. Loosen your grip enough to let them twist. To do this, continue holding the loop end firmly, and slowly slide your other hand toward your helper, letting the strands twist as you go. Your helper can continue to pull on the other end of the lariat so that the spirals fall into place.

9. Your yarn lariat should be at least 3 feet long, and it's now ready for tying knots in the next activity. Later, to wear it as a belt, simply run it through your belt loops and tie the ends. You can cut the belt to shorten it, but most people prefer to let the ends hang.

PROJECT KNOT KNOW-HOW

Cowboys used lariats and other ropes for a lot of their work, and that meant that they had to know what kind of knot to use for each task. For example, they used one knot called a "honda" to turn their lariat into a lasso for roping cattle, but then used a different knot to tie the other end of the lariat to the saddle horn. Whether tying a pack, pulling a string of ponies, or securing a guide rope across a river, cowboys knew which of the knots would hold without slipping.

When cowboys were riding the range or sitting around the cook's fire, they often practiced tying knots and tried to invent new ones. They even had contests to see who could tie a knot that the others could not copy.

In this activity, you can try your hand at some of the most common cowboy knots. Either use your lariat from the previous project or use a piece of clothesline. The best way to learn to tie a particular knot is to study the picture and repeat what is shown. Once you know how to tie a knot, practice it a few times and it will soon become so easy that you can tie it without looking.

MATERIALS
lariat from the previous project, or about 3 feet of clothesline or other cord

a post or railing
bandanna, or any large square of cloth

Half Hitch

A knot that is used to tie a rope to some object, like a post or a tree is called a "hitch." The half hitch is the simplest form of hitch. Many cowboys used the half hitch to fasten their lariats to the saddle horn.

1. When you tie your shoes, or tie string on a package, the first knot you tie is called an overhand knot. Tie an overhand knot around a post or railing.

2. Slip the end of the rope through the loop you formed, then pull on the rope to tighten it.

half hitch

Hitching Post Knot

Just about everyone on the western frontier used this knot to tie the horse's reins to a hitching post or railing.

1. Start the same as you did with the half hitch, but form a second loop with the end of the rope.

2. Pull the end of the rope through the second loop. Pull on the rope to tighten it.

hitching post knot

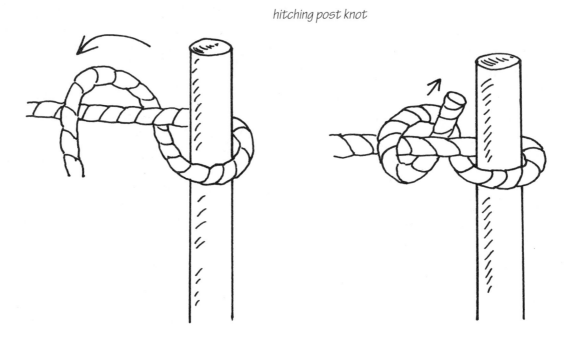

Clove Hitch

When branding a calf or breaking a wild horse, cowboys used the clove hitch to tie the end of the lariat to a post. This was a temporary hitch that would work loose with constant tugging. It was just right for quick tasks and could be detached speedily simply by lifting the loops off the post.

1. Pass the end of the rope around a post or railing, then cross the end over the long part of the rope to form a loop.

2. Pass the rope around the post again to make a second loop and pull the end up under the rope.

3. Pull on the long end of the rope to tighten the knot.

clove hitch

step 1

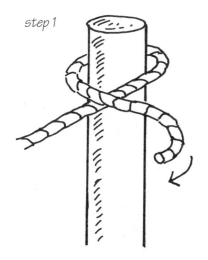

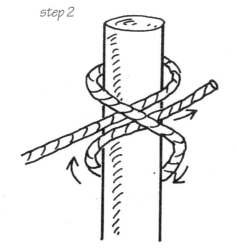

step 2

Wild Horses

Hundreds of wild horses roamed the West in the late 1800s, often mixing with horses that had run away from ranches, cattle drives, or army forts. Frontier people called these wild horses different names: mustangs (from the Spanish word *mesteno*); broncos (from the Spanish word *broncho*); or *cayuse*, after the Cayuse tribe, well known for their horses. Ranchers often rounded up the broncos, then usually hired a skilled bronco buster to tame them. In 1872, ranchers held a contest of bronco busting and steer roping in Cheyenne that is believed to be the start of modern rodeos.

Neckerchief Knot

Cowboys wore their bandannas, or "wipes" in cowboy language, in front, with the knot in back. They could then pull the neckerchief up quickly to cover the nose and mouth to block out dust or strong wind.

1. Fold the bandanna, or other cloth, in half to form a triangle.

2. Tie the ends in an overhand knot.

3. Now tie a second overhand knot going the other way. If your knot looks square, or like a figure 8, you've tied a square knot, which is exactly what the cowboys used. If the knot doesn't look square, you've simply tied a double knot, which doesn't hold as well and can be harder to untie. If this happens, try again.

neckerchief knot

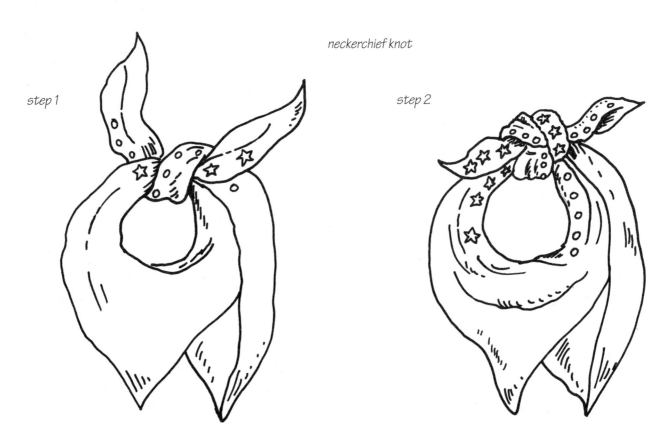

step 1

step 2

CHAPTER FOUR

Winter

Work on the Thayer ranch slowed down during the winter months, although there was still plenty to do. Pa and the cowboys took turns as "outriders," riding over the ranch property and the open range to check on the cattle. They had to keep on guard against rustlers and make sure no cattle strayed too far from the ranch. During heavy storms, they drove the herd into sheltered valleys and ravines for protection. When they weren't tending the cattle, Pa and the cowboys spent time cleaning and repairing equipment.

While Amy and Tom continued their daily chores, they had more time for schoolwork. They also found time to have fun, either indoors or out. The family visited neighbors, too, even though the closest ranch was two miles away, and they made several trips into Cheyenne.

LESSONS FROM KIP

All the cowboys were friendly toward the Thayer children, but Kip spent more time with them than any of the others did. He sometimes told them stories about his adventures as a cowboy, including several gun battles with bands of Indian warriors. He did not say much about his life as a slave, but he did share many African folktales and riddles he had learned from his parents.

Kip was skilled at making things. With help from Pa and two of the cowboys, he built a small shed attached to the bunkhouse to use as a workshop. Amy and Tom often watched him making things there, like a set of stirrups for one of the cowboys and a dinner bell for Miguel. He showed Amy how to make a bead necklace like the ones worn by Indian women and men. And he helped the children make a board game he called Mustang and Cowboys and a puzzle called a buttonhole puzzle.

PROJECT BUTTONHOLE PUZZLE

Americans on the frontier made a variety of simple-looking devices called "hand puzzles." They made the puzzles out of scraps of material—a piece of wood, some string, and a couple of beads or rings. Even though the puzzles were easy to make, some of them were almost impossible to solve. In this project, you can make and try the simplest form of one called the buttonhole puzzle. Try to figure out the puzzle on your own before you look at the solution.

MATERIALS
piece of poster board or stiff cardboard, 1¼-by-5 inches
ruler
pencil
scissors
hole punch
piece of string, about 36 inches long
button, 1 inch or more in diameter, with at least 2 holes

1. With the hole punch, make a hole about ½ inch in from each end of the cardboard. Use the punch several times to enlarge each hole, but make sure your button won't fit through the holes.

2. Fold the string in half and push the loop end through one hole. Run the two ends of the string through the loop, then through the other hole, as shown in the diagram.

3. Tie the ends of the string to the button.

4. Now see if you can remove the string from the cardboard. Try it different ways before you look at the solution.

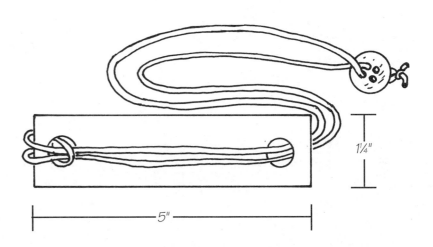

African American Cowboys

When the Civil War brought an end to slavery in the United States, many former slaves joined the westward movement. Families went west as homesteaders or to start businesses, and many young African American men went in search of adventure. Some joined the United States Army; an even greater number became cowboys. By the 1870s, about one out of every seven cowboys was an African American. Probably the most famous of these cowboys was Nat Love. Love was so skilled at riding and roping that he became one of the first stars of the rodeo shows after the days of the long cattle drives ended.

The Solution

1. Arrange the puzzle so it looks like the drawing for assembling the puzzle.

2. Grip the loop at the left and pull it down through the hole at the right. Keep pulling through the right-hand hole, making a large loop, as shown in the diagram.

3. Pull that large loop up over the left side of the puzzle. Pull on the button and the string will pull free. You should be able to reverse the solution to set up the puzzle again. If you can't, untie the string and start over.

The solution

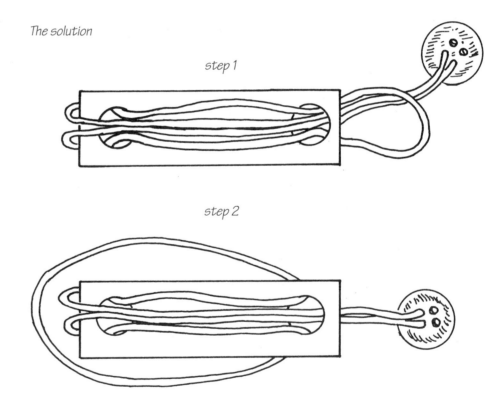

step 1

step 2

MUSTANG AND COWBOYS BOARD GAME

People on the Wild West frontier were fond of all sorts of board games. On long winter evenings, families often sat around a warm fire or woodstove and played games by the light of kerosene or oil lanterns. Traditional games like checkers, chess, and Parcheesi were popular, and people invented dozens of new board games in the late 1800s.

In this project, you'll make a version of a popular hunt game. The game had several different names, including mustang and cowboys. The object of the game is for cowboys to trap the mustang so that it can't move, but the mustang wins if it jumps over all the cowboys except one. By using a small box for your game board, you'll have a portable game you can take on trips, with the game pieces stored inside.

MATERIALS

several sheets of newspaper
small, sturdy cardboard box, about 6 inches square
  (Size can vary; a gift box or box in which greeting cards are sold will work well.)
ruler
pencil
large nail or compass point
14 golf tees (13 of an identical color, 1 tee must be a different color)

marking pen (if needed to color 1 tee)
poster paint, any color (optional, for painting the box)
  small paintbrush (optional)
2 players

1. If you plan to paint the box, spread several sheets of newspaper over your work surface. If the box surface is plain, you don't have to paint it, but you will want to use paint to cover lettering or designs. Use any color you wish, and apply a second coat after the first dries (about 1 hour).

2. Use a ruler and pencil to mark dots in the box lid for 33 holes, arranging the dots in crossing rows of 7, as shown in the drawing. Space the dots ¾ inch apart. (If the box is 6 inches square, make the first dot ¾ inch in from each edge; this will center the pattern in the middle of the square.)

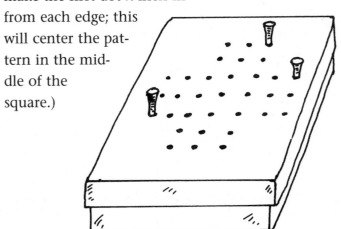

3. Use a compass point or nail to make a hole at each of the 33 dots. The holes should be just large enough for a golf tee to fit in snugly.

4. If necessary, use paint or a marking pen to make 1 tee a different color from the others. This tee, or game piece, will be the mustang, so the color must stand out distinctly.

5. Place the thirteen cowboy game pieces and the single mustang piece in the game board following the pattern shown in the diagram. You're now ready to play mustang and cowboys.

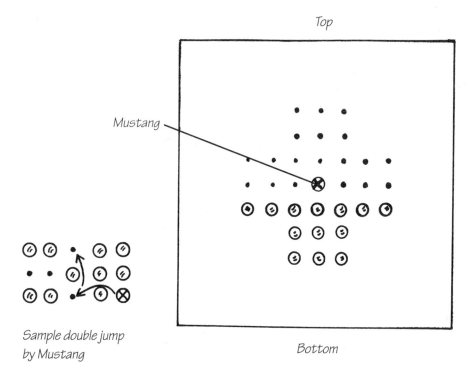

Sample double jump by Mustang

Rules for Mustang and Cowboys

1. One player moves the cowboys, the other moves only the mustang. The players take turns, with one of the cowboys making the first move.

2. A cowboy can move up the board or across (left or right) one space at a time to a vacant hole. But the cowboys cannot move down, toward the bottom of the board.

3. The mustang can move one space at a time, up or down the board, or across (left or right) to a vacant hole. No diagonal moves are allowed for any game piece.

4. The mustang can "jump" a cowboy by going over the cowboy game piece to a vacant hole. (No long jumps of more than one space are allowed, but double jumps are okay as long as there is a vacant hole in between.) When a cowboy piece is jumped, it is removed from the board.

5. The cowboys cannot jump over each other or over the mustang. They win only if they trap the mustang so that it cannot make a move.

6. Play continues until (a) the mustang is trapped, (b) all the cowboys except one have been removed, or (c) neither side can make any more moves.

PROJECT BEAD NECKLACE

The first Americans to explore the Far West were the hunters and trappers known as "mountain men." They always took along a supply of glass beads for trading with the Native American tribes. The men and women of every tribe were skilled in making bead jewelry and decorations. Before they had glass beads, they made beads from bits of bone, antler, seashell, and semiprecious stones, drilling holes with a stone-tipped drill. The glass beads brought by the mountain men, and by later pioneers and traders, were a welcome addition to their supplies. Native Americans used the tiniest beads, called seed beads, to sew colorful decorations on clothing, headdresses, parfleches, and other objects. They used larger beads to make necklaces, bracelets, and other items of jewelry.

In this project, you can use common household items to make your own version of a Native American bead necklace. You'll make some beads out of macaroni, others out of colored paper.

MATERIALS
several sheets of newspaper
small bowl
teaspoon
¼ cup rubbing alcohol
red and blue food coloring
10 to 12 pieces of macaroni
2 or 3 paper towels
2 6-inch squares of colored paper, such as wrapping paper or construction paper
ruler
pencil
scissors
knitting needle, chopstick, or handle of an artist's paintbrush
white glue
18 to 20 inches of string or dental floss

1. Spread several sheets of newspaper over your work surface.

2. Pour 5 or 6 teaspoons of rubbing alcohol into a small bowl. Add a few drops of red food coloring—just enough to make a rich red color.

3. Place 5 or 6 pieces of macaroni into the colored alcohol. Stir the macaroni with the teaspoon for 5 or 10 seconds.

4. Pour off the alcohol and put the red macaroni on a paper towel to dry. (Drying will take only a minute or two.)

5. Rinse out the bowl and repeat steps 2 to 4 to make 5 or 6 blue macaroni beads. Set the beads aside.

6. Place a ruler along the top edge of a 6-inch paper square and make pencil marks 1 inch apart across the top, as shown in the diagram. Do the same along the bottom edge of the paper.

7. Use the diagram as a model to draw lines dividing the paper into triangles. Simply draw your lines to every other inch mark, as shown. Cut out the five large triangles.

8. Repeat steps 6 and 7 with a different color paper.

9. Roll the wide end of a paper triangle around a knitting needle or similar object. Keep rolling until you get to the point of the triangle.

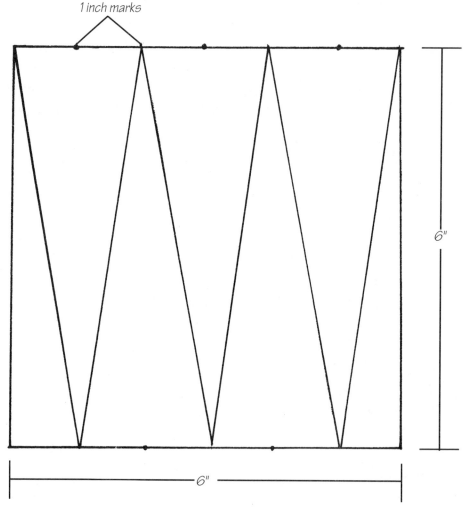

1 inch marks

6"

6"

10. Place a few drops of glue on the triangle point and fix it to the rest of the paper bead. Remove the knitting needle.

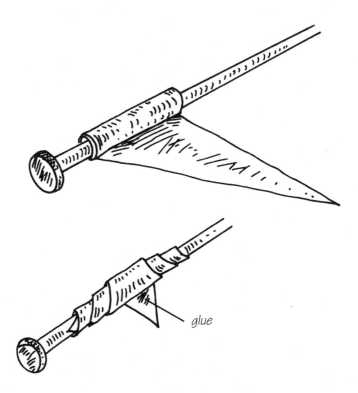

glue

11. Repeat steps 9 and 10 with the other triangles.

12. String the paper and macaroni beads on a piece of string or dental floss. Make any arrangement of shapes and colors that looks pleasing to you.

13. Tie the ends of the string in a firm double knot or a square knot. Your bead necklace is ready to wear.

AMY TAKES CHARGE

Early in the winter, Miguel went with Ma and Pa Thayer for a day trip to Cheyenne to buy supplies. Since there was no snow on the ground, they took the ranch wagon rather than a sleigh. But a sudden blizzard swept in from the mountains and they found themselves snowbound in town. It was four days before they made it back to the ranch.

With Miguel and Ma away, Amy was in charge of preparing meals for those four days. She didn't worry about her parents or Miguel because people were often stranded when traveling in winter. But she did worry about how to make enough food for five hungry cowboys and her two brothers. Kip helped out by making lots of strong coffee, the way the ranch hands liked it. Tom helped with the cooking and baking, and Tad scrubbed the long table before and after the meals.

Amy did everything else herself, even though she found that she was in the kitchen almost constantly from before dawn until after dark. When she

wasn't cooking or planning meals, she worked on a yarn picture she was making as a Christmas present for her parents. The ranch hands seemed to enjoy all of her meals, and they said her biscuits were every bit as good as Miguel's. Amy decided the two dishes that came out best were her scrambled eggs, served with steaks, and her corn chowder.

PROJECT CORN CHOWDER

When the first European colonists arrived in North America, they were amazed to discover that the Native Americans enjoyed many foods that Europeans had never seen or tasted. These New World foods included corn, beans, squash, turkey, cranberries, and many others that are now used throughout the world. When the Pilgrims prepared the first feast of thanksgiving in 1621, they served the foods they had learned about from the Native Americans.

As Americans moved westward in the 1800s, they found that many of the tribes planted corn, beans, and squash. These three vegetables became known as the "three sisters," because they always seemed to be grown together. On the Great Plains, some of the tribes did not plant any crops because all of their food was gotten by hunting and gathering wild foods, but many others relied on the three sisters. One of the favorite meals in these tribes was corn stew, or chowder. The recipe you'll follow is a modern version of this popular dish.

INGREDIENTS

1 small onion
½ green pepper
1 medium potato
4 tablespoons butter or margarine
½ teaspoon salt
dash of pepper
1 1-pound can whole-kernel corn
1 1-pound can creamed corn
*1 teaspoon parsley flakes, or 2 tablespoons minced
    fresh parsley*
2½ cups milk

EQUIPMENT

measuring cups and spoons
paring knife (to be used by an adult)
cutting board
potato peeler
*food processor or food chopper (optional, to be used
    with an adult)*
large saucepan (2 to 4 quarts)
mixing spoon
adult helper

MAKES

4 to 5 servings

1. Peel the onion (under cold running water to prevent tears).

2. Have your adult helper use a paring knife to core the green pepper. Remove the seeds.

Frontier Women

Life for girls and women on the western frontier was far different from life in the more settled regions of the East. Frontier women often did the same work as men, especially when a family was just getting started on a homestead or ranch. Many farm women plowed the fields with their husbands. On some ranches, women and teenage girls often rode the range or helped with roundups and branding. Several women owned ranches—Elizabeth Morley of Colorado was known as the "cattle queen" because of the large ranch she operated. Other women helped in family businesses or operated remote mail pickups on the railroad lines.

In 1869, when Wyoming became a territory (the first step in becoming a state), the territorial government allowed women to vote—something they couldn't do anywhere else in the United States. When Wyoming was admitted to the Union as a state in 1890, it became the first state with voting rights for women.

3. Peel the potato, then ask the adult to use a paring knife, food processor, or food chopper to dice (cut into small pieces) the potato, onion, and green pepper.

4. Have the adult helper melt the butter or margarine in a large saucepan. Add the potato, onion, and green pepper.

5. Sauté (cook over low heat) the ingredients for 10 to 12 minutes, or until the diced potato is becoming tender. Stir frequently with the mixing spoon as you sauté.

6. With the heat still on low, add the salt, pepper, and both cans of corn.

7. Stir in the parsley, then slowly stir in the milk.

8. Ask the adult to heat the chowder to the boiling point (but don't boil), then lower the heat to simmer for about 5 minutes. Stir occasionally. Serve your corn chowder hot with bread or rolls.

PROJECT RANCH SCRAMBLED EGGS

Cooking on the Wild West frontier was influenced by the cooking of Mexico, the Hispanic Southwest, and the Native American tribes of the Southwest, like the Navajo and Hopi. In this style of cooking, people used a lot of spices and peppers, both red and green. Some Southwestern dishes were so hot or spicy that anyone trying them for the first time was likely to rush to the water well to cool their mouths. The recipe you'll follow, however, is very mild. If you want to make the dish hotter, add the paprika and chili powder.

INGREDIENTS
6 eggs
¼ cup milk
1 small onion
1 small or ½ large green pepper
¾ cup diced cooked ham
½ teaspoon salt
⅛ to ¼ teaspoon pepper
⅛ teaspoon paprika (optional)
⅛ teaspoon chili powder (optional)
3 tablespoons butter, margarine, or cooking oil
¾ cup Monterey Jack or cheddar cheese

EQUIPMENT
large mixing bowl
measuring cups and spoons
eggbeater
paring knife (to be used by an adult)
cutting board
food processor or food chopper (optional)
mixing spoon
large skillet
fork
spatula
cheese grater
adult helper

MAKES
4 to 5 servings

1. Crack the eggs into a large mixing bowl. Wash your hands after handling the raw eggs.

2. Add the milk and beat with an eggbeater until the mixture is smooth and light yellow in color.

3. Have the adult dice the onion, green pepper, and ham with a paring knife and cutting board, or food processor or chopper.

4. Add the onion, green pepper, and ham to the eggs. Stir well with a mixing spoon to blend the ingredients.

5. Add the salt and pepper. If you want to use paprika and chili powder, add them now. Stir well.

6. Ask the adult to heat the butter, margarine, or oil in a large skillet over low to medium heat.

7. Pour the egg mixture into the hot skillet. As the scrambled eggs cook, stir them several times with a fork. Use a spatula if the eggs begin to stick to the pan.

8. Continue cooking, with occasional stirring, until the eggs are done the way you like them, either moist or cooked longer until they are dry.

9. Use a cheese grater to grate the cheese directly onto the eggs. Serve warm.

PROJECT YARN PICTURE

Hispanic settlers in what is now the American Southwest brought with them from Mexico the art of making yarn pictures. The pictures, which are still made today, are called *ofrendas*, meaning "offerings" or "gifts." Artists make *ofrendas* on thin boards. They cover the boards with soft wax, then press brightly colored yarns into the wax to form a picture. The pictures are often of animals, but plants and abstract designs are also fairly common. For your yarn picture, you'll apply the yarn with glue, rather than wax. You'll find that *ofrendas* are fun to work on and make an attractive display. Hang your finished picture on the wall of your room.

MATERIALS
several sheets of newspaper
poster board, any color, or stiff cardboard
ruler
pencil
scissors
assorted yarn in bright colors (including scraps from other projects)
white glue
transparent tape or masking tape

1. Spread several sheets of newspaper on your work surface and place the poster board or cardboard on it.

2. Use ruler and pencil to measure 6-by-8 inch rectangle. Cut out the rectangle with scissors.

3. Draw the outline of an animal on the poster board in pencil. Either use the butterfly pattern shown here or create your own. You might want to draw a cat, dog, or some other favorite animal, but keep the drawing simple.

4. Place a single strand of yarn on part of the outline you drew (it doesn't have to reach all the way around). Lift up the yarn and make a thin line of glue on the outline where you are placing the strand. Press the yarn onto the wet glue.

Tips: Always press the yarn gently into the glue. This helps to keep the yarn fluffy. Try to handle the yarn gently at all times.

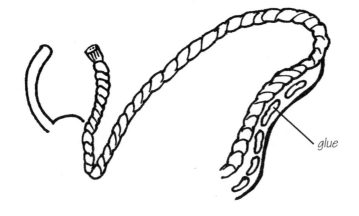

glue

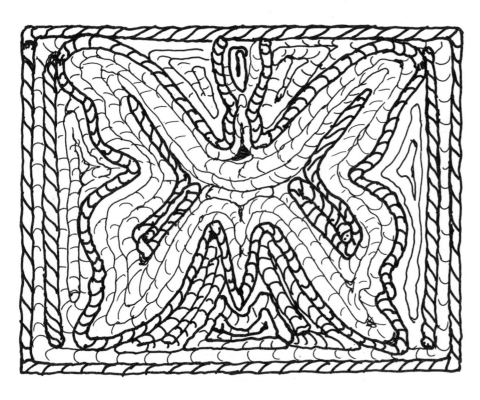

5. Continue gluing a single strand all the way around the outline. Change colors or strands anytime you wish. Simply start the new strand where the previous strand ends.

6. Fill in the figure with strands of yarn in the same way, applying glue and yarn a little at a time. Work from the outside toward the center. Keep the strands as close together as possible, so that the strands touch each other and there is no bare space showing.

7. You can use little scraps of yarn to fill in any spaces in the center of the figure.

8. Fill in the background just as you did the figure. First, make a single strand all the way around the outside, then work strand by strand toward the figure.

9. For hanging your finished picture, cut a 4-inch piece of yarn. Center it on the back of the poster board about one-fourth of the way down from the top edge. Use a piece of tape to fix each end of the yarn to the poster board. Slip the yarn over a picture hook or tack on your wall.

THE CHRISTMAS SEASON

Christmas on the Thayer ranch was a happy, busy season, as it was for most families on the Wild West frontier. Two of the cowboys rode into the mountains to cut down a Christmas tree for the ranch house and another for the bunkhouse. One of the cowboys took the train east to visit his parents, but for the other ranch hands, the Thayers had become their family.

Tom and Amy had fun making presents and decorations. Tom made a toy called a chromatrope for Tad, and Amy made beautiful straw stars to decorate the tree. Ma helped them make a large clay piñata, which they filled with candies and trinkets, then hung from a ceiling beam. On Christmas Eve, everyone took a turn trying to break open the clay pot with a stick. They all made sure to fail so that it would be Tad who would smash the piñata on his second try and send the treasures tumbling to the floor.

Pa and the cowboys went on a hunting trip to bring back wild game, including a deer and turkeys, for the Christmas feast. After the meal, they sat around the big ranch house table and talked about how the frontier was changing. More settlers were arriving every year, and towns like Cheyenne were growing fast. They all said they hoped the Indian wars were over and that Indians and settlers would now learn to live at peace with one another.

PARTY PIÑATA

Piñatas were first made in Europe more than 400 years ago. The Spanish brought the idea to the New World in the 1500s, and Hispanic settlers from Mexico continued the custom in the American Southwest. Until modern times, people made piñatas out of thin clay filled with candy and small toys. At Christmas, or other holiday celebrations, the party guests took turns being blindfolded and whacking at the piñata with a stick. When they clay pot was finally smashed, all the goodies tumbled out.

In this project, you'll use a simple form of papier-mâché to make your piñata. Papier-mâché is a mixture of paper and paste, and it's what most modern piñatas are made from. This is an ambitious project, with drying times that can take up to a week. But you'll find it's fun to work on. You might want to plan making the piñata with a friend, as well as an adult helper. The three cone shapes on your piñata stand for the Three Wise Men who, in the Bible, carried gifts to the infant Jesus. If you want a different shape for other celebrations, like a birthday party, Hanukkah, or Kwanza, you can easily turn the basic piñata into a clown's head or an animal. Use just one cone as a clown's hat, or two cones for horns on a cow.

MATERIALS

10 to 12 sheets of newspaper
smock or apron
medium saucepan (2 to 4 quarts)
tap water
½ cup flour
mixing spoon
balloon
string, about 48 inches, plus 1 long piece for hanging
scissors
transparent tape
1 sheet construction paper, any color
ruler
pencil
4 or 5 sheets colored tissue paper
craft knife or paring knife (to be used by an adult)
about 24 prizes (wrapped candies, trinkets, small toys)
adult helper

1. Spread 4 or 5 sheets of newspaper over your work surface. This can be a messy project, so it's a good idea to wear a smock or apron.

2. Pour 7 cups of water into the saucepan. Slowly stir in the flour.

3. Ask an adult helper to heat the paste mixture on the stove to a gentle boil. Cook and stir the mixture until it becomes smooth and creamy. Set the paste aside to cool.

4. While the paste cools, blow up the balloon until it is about 8 inches from top to bottom and tie it.

5. Tear 4 or 5 sheets of newspaper into small strips, about 1-by-4 inches.

6. When the paste is cool enough to work with, dip strips of newspaper into the paste. Wipe the excess paste off by running the strip between your thumb and pointer finger, then lay each strip onto the balloon. Overlap the strips so the balloon doesn't show through. Cover the balloon with two layers of these strips, placing the second layer in a different direction.

7. Make a harness for the piñata by cutting four 12-inch pieces of string. Tie the pieces together in the middle to make a large X. Place the X on your work surface and position the balloon in the middle. Bring the ends of the string up and tie them together at the top of the balloon. Tie a long piece of string to the knot at the top of the piñata for hanging. Tape the strings to the sides of the balloon to hold them in place.

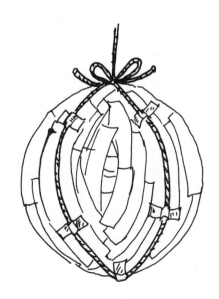

8. Apply two more layers of the pasted newspaper strips, covering the strings. Hang the piñata to dry. This will take 3 days.

9. To make three cones for your piñata, begin by measuring and cutting an 8-inch square of colored construction paper. Use a drawing compass to draw a circle 8 inches in diameter on the square, then divide the circle into 4 pie-shaped quarters, as shown in the diagram. Cut out the 4 pie shapes.

10. Form three of the pie-shaped pieces into cones, as shown in the diagram, holding the seam in place with transparent tape. Tape the three cones at an equal distance from each other on the sides of the balloon about ⅓ of the way from the top.

11. Ask your adult helper to cut three sides of a small door near the top of the piñata with a craft knife or paring knife. This will pop the balloon. Pull out the balloon if you can, or let it drop to the bottom of the piñata.

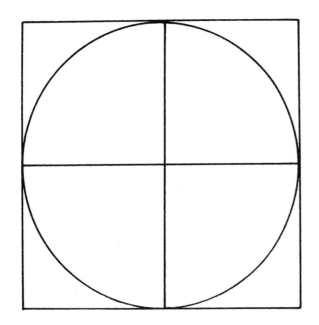

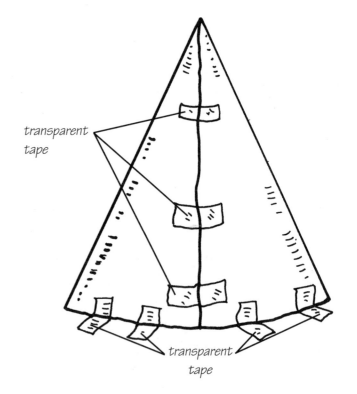

transparent tape

transparent tape

12. Fill the piñata with treasures, then seal the edges of the door with tape.

13. Cut the sheets of tissue paper into long strips, about 3 inches wide and 6 to 8 inches long. Place several strips on top of each other and cut fringes in them. Make the cuts about 1/2 inch apart and about half the width of the strip.

14. Apply single layers of the fringed tissue paper to the piñata by applying a little paste to the solid part of the tissue paper (not the fringe). Paste the tissue paper in overlapping rows around the piñata, cutting the paper where necessary to fit around the cones. The fringes should all point down.

Tip: Tissue paper tends to bleed when it's wet, so you'll want to be careful to avoid drips.

15. Hang the piñata to dry for 2 or 3 days and get ready for your party!

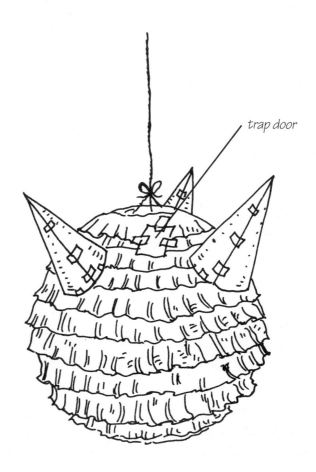

trap door

PROJECT · CHROMATROPE TOY

In the 1800s, Americans became fascinated with a variety of toys that created optical illusions (seeing something that wasn't really there). Some of the toys gave the illusion of movement. Others, like the chromatrope, produced changing patterns or colors. The toy inventor often gave the device a fancy, scientific-sounding name, like "phenakistoscope." The chromatrope, for example, was also known as the "kaleidoscopic chromatrope" and as the "philosophical whiz-gig." While toy manufacturers made elaborate versions of the toys, many children figured out how to make their own. In this project, you'll make the simplest form of chromatrope, one that was invented in 1875. You can also use the toy as a "kaleidoscopic top."

MATERIALS

several sheets of newspaper

white poster board, or stiff cardboard, about 3 inches square

drawing compass, or any round object about 3 inches in diameter

scissors

crayons, colored pencils, or felt-tip pens (red, white, and blue)

nail or compass point, if needed

thin, strong string

wooden pencil, about 3 inches long

1. Spread several sheets of newspaper over your work surface and place the poster board on top.

2. Use a drawing compass, glass, or any other round object to draw a circle on the poster board, about 3 inches in diameter. Cut out the circle with scissors.

3. Use a pencil to copy pattern 1 onto one side of your circle. Start in the center at A and draw a swirl from the center point to the outside of the circle, as shown in the diagram. Draw lightly at first so you can correct mistakes. Make a second swirling line starting in the center at B.

4. Use red crayon, colored pencil, or felt-tip pen to color lines A and B. Follow your pencil line, but make the red lines fairly wide, as indicated in the diagram.

5. Use a ruler and pencil to copy pattern 2 onto the other side of the circle. If you make all the sides of the large triangles 2½ inches long, the pattern will look like the picture. Color the pattern red, white, and blue as indicated.

Pattern 1

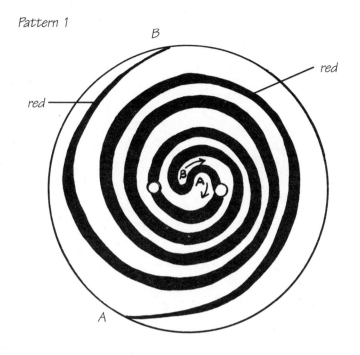

red

red

B

A

Pattern 2

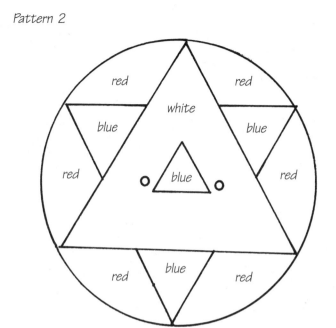

red red

white

blue blue

red blue red

red blue red

6. With the compass point or a nail, make two small holes in the circle, ¾ inch apart. (Each hole will be ⅜ inch from the center point.)

7. Cut a piece of string about 40 inches long. Thread the string through the two holes, then tie the ends together in a firm double knot or a square knot.

8. Slide the circle to the middle of the string. Pick up the string by the ends, slipping the loops over your pointer fingers, as shown in the picture.

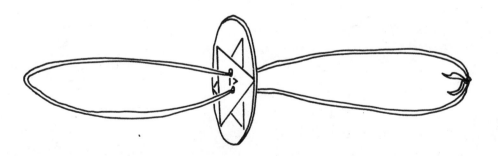

9. To wind up the chromatrope, swing it over and over until the string is wound tightly.

Home Entertainment

The chromatrope was just one of many devices that people used for home entertainment in the late 1800s. Many families owned a stereoscope, for example, a device for looking at two photographs placed side by side. When the viewer looked through the lens, the picture suddenly emerged in three dimensions.

Magic lanterns were another popular entertainment device. The magic lantern was a simple box with a lantern inside that projected a picture onto a wall or screen. Several other inventions gave the viewer the illusion of seeing moving pictures. These devices, with names like "zoetrope" and "phantascope," were revolving drums with slits in the side. On the inside of the drum, a flexible card stretched all the way around. The card contained a sequence of 20 or 30 pictures, such as a horse running. As the viewer turned the drum and looked through the slits, the horse seemed to be in motion. By changing the circular picture card, a family could spend an evening watching this early form of motion pictures.

10. Hold your hands at the same height, so the chromatrope is straight up and down. Slowly pull your hands apart. As the toy spins and unwinds, watch the colors and patterns change.

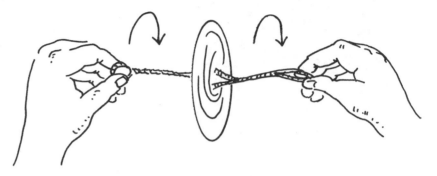

To Make a Kaleidoscopic Top

1. To turn your chromatrope into a top, first remove the string from the two holes.

2. Poke a short pencil (about 3 inches long) through the exact center of the chromatrope. If you used a drawing compass to make your circle, the hole is already started. Push only about ½ inch of the pencil through the hole.

3. Hold the pencil by the eraser and spin the top to watch the patterns and colors.

4. Put the pencil through the other way to watch the second pattern.

STRAW STAR

As American pioneers moved west, they carried with them the customs of their former homes in the East or in other parts of the world. This included customs for holidays like Christmas. Around 1800, for example, immigrants from Germany brought their homeland tradition of decorating Christmas trees, and the practice soon spread throughout the country. Pioneers who came from Norway and Sweden followed their custom of making tree decorations out of straw. They made straw figures of people and animals, and one of their most popular decorations was a straw star. The star was an important symbol in the New Testament of the Bible, because a mysterious star guided the shepherds and the three wise men to the infant Jesus. The six-pointed star is also called the Star of David, a symbol of the Jewish religion, and appears on the flag of Israel.

Easy to make, straw stars are attractive as tree decorations or as ornaments to hang in a window. You can buy straw at craft and hobby stores, florists, and even many produce stands, particularly in autumn. If necessary, you can substitute reeds, cattails, or dried grasses you pick yourself (with permission if they're on someone's property). You can even make these stars out of twigs or drinking straws.

MATERIALS

10 to 12 long pieces of straw or similar material
roasting pan or dish pan
tap water
several paper towels
scissors
red thread, about 36 inches
white glue or craft glue (optional)

1. Place the straw, reeds, or grasses in a pan of lukewarm tap water. Soak for 10 minutes.

2. Remove the straw from the water and pat it dry with paper towels.

3. With scissors, cut the straw into equal lengths—about 4 inches. You'll need two strands for each side of the star, so cut a total of 12 4-inch strands.

4. Form a triangle with 6 pieces of straw (2 pieces for each side). Overlap the ends a little, as indicated in the picture.

5. When you have the triangle laid out, cut 3 pieces of red thread (each about 4 inches long).

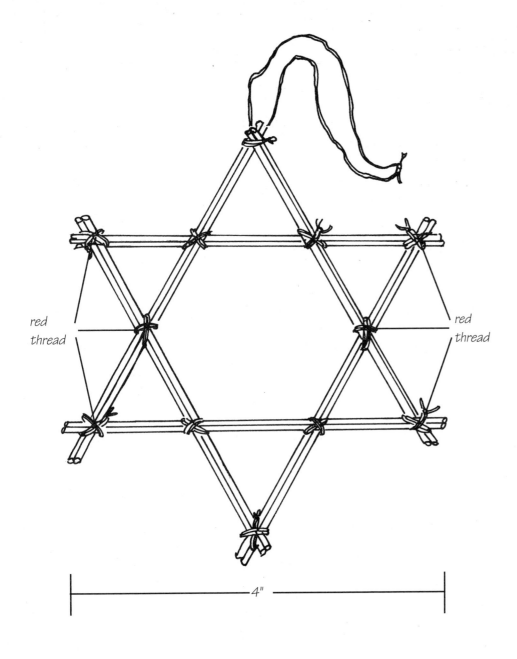

red
thread

red
thread

4"

Wrap the thread in a criss-cross around the straw ends two or three times, then tie it in a double knot.

6. You can add a few drops of glue under the thread and on the knot to make the connection stronger if you wish.

7. Make a second triangle the same way.

8. Place one triangle on top of the other, as shown in the picture.

9. Tie the two triangles together with red thread at each of the six points where the triangles meet. Seal the connections with a touch of glue for added strength, if you wish.

10. Tie a 4- or 5-inch length of thread to the top of the star for hanging. Your six-sided star is finished.

GLOSSARY

Acoma　A Native American tribe living in what is now the Southwestern United States, famous for their beautiful pottery.

adobe　Building material made of sun-dried mud, often formed into bricks, and widely used in desert regions.

Apache　A Native American tribe living in what is now the Southwest of the United States and northern Mexico.

boom town　A town that grew up rapidly, usually a mining town or a town where a cattle trail met a railroad line.

branding　Marking cattle or horses with a hot iron that imprints the symbol of the owner on the animal's hide.

bronco　A wild horse.

bronco buster　A cowboy who had special skill in taming wild horses.

cattle drive　The movement of a herd of cattle from ranches and grazing lands to the railroad lines for shipment to meat-packing plants farther east.

cayuse A wild horse, named after the Cayuse tribe, which was famous for its horses.

chamois Soft leather cloth made of deerskin or other animal hide.

chaps Long leather leggings worn by cowboys over their pants for protection against cactus and other range plants.

Cheyenne A group of Native American tribes living in the Great Plains region.

chromatrope A spinning toy that creates changing patterns and colors as it spins.

chuck wagon The cooking and supply wagon used by ranch cooks during roundups and cattle drives.

clove hitch A knot used by cowboys to tie a rope or lariat to a post.

cutting horse A ranch horse specially trained to single out (or "cut") a steer or horse from a herd.

Dutch oven A large iron pot used for baking over an open fire.

frijoles refritos A Spanish term for "refried beans," a favorite recipe in the American Southwest and in Mexico.

fruit leather Fruit that has been dried, either in the sun or in an oven, to preserve it for long periods.

Great Plains A region of prairie, or tall grasses, located between the Mississippi River and the Rocky Mountains.

half hitch A knot often used by cowboys to tie a lariat to the saddle horn.

Hispanic Of Spanish origin.

hitch A knot used to tie a rope to something else, like a post or railing.

homesteaders Settlers on the Great Plains who were granted land at very little cost, provided that they lived on the land.

Hopi A Native American tribe living in what is now the Southwest of the United States, famous for their craftwork.

horno A beehive-shaped adobe oven used by the Pueblo tribes of the Southwest.

jerky Strips of dried meat that could be stored for long periods.

kiln A special oven used to heat clay at high temperatures in order to harden it.

lariat A braided rope used by cowboys.

lasso   A lariat tied with a special knot so that the lariat could be tightened when thrown over the head of a steer or horse.

longhorns   Cattle with very long horns that originally ran wild in much of Texas and northern Mexico until rounded up by ranchers and cowboys for the great cattle drives of the Wild West.

magic lantern   A popular device in the 1800s used to project a picture onto a wall or screen.

mountain men   Hunters and trappers who were the first Americans to explore the Great Plains and Rocky Mountains in the early 1800s.

mustang   A wild horse.

Navajo   A large Native American tribe living in what is now New Mexico, Arizona, and southern Utah.

New World   What the Europeans called North and South America.

ofrenda   Spanish for "offering" or "gift;" a yarn picture made by Hispanic crafts-people.

owner stick   A stick decorated with symbols, used to mark the belongings of the family whose symbols were on the stick.

pemmican   A mixture of dried meat with fruits and nuts made by Native Americans to create a nutritious meal that could be carried or stored for many months.

pinwheel   A toy with fins that turn in a breeze like a miniature windmill.

Plains Indian   Any of the tribes living on the Great Plains, many of which depended on the great herds of buffalo roaming that region.

poke   A pouch or bag used by cowboys to carry small personal items.

prairie   An area of tall grasses and few trees.

pueblo   The houses of the Native American tribes of the Southwest, usually made of adobe.

range   An open area of grassland where cattle and horses grazed.

range wars   Conflicts in the Wild West over range land, with cattle ranchers fighting farmers, sheep ranchers, or other cattle ranchers.

rawhide   A strip of leather or animal hide.

remuda   The Spanish word for "change" or "replacement," used for a small herd of horses, usually referring to the horses on a cattle drive or a ranch.

reservations   Land set aside by the United States government where Native American tribes were forced to live.

rodeo   A display of skill in bronco busting and roping that began in the 1870s and remains popular in the West today.

ropewalk   A long, narrow shop where skilled rope makers braided strands of hemp or other material into rope.

roundup   The bringing together of a ranch's cattle for branding or to start a cattle drive.

saddle band   Another term for a *remuda*, the band of horses on a ranch or cattle drive.

seed beads   Tiny colored beads used by many Native American tribes to decorate clothing and other items, or to make jewelry.

scurvy   A disease caused by lack of vitamin C contained in fruits and vegetables.

Sioux   A group of Native American tribes living on the Great Plains who fiercely resisted being forced onto reservations in the late 1800s.

sod   The thick soil and matted grass of a prairie.

sourdough starter Material used for baking bread when yeast was not available.

territory A region of the United States that has not become a state but has its own government similar to that of a state.

transcontinental railroad A railroad that stretched across the continent from the Mississippi River to the West Coast, with the first one completed in 1869.

vaquero The Spanish word for cowboy.

wo-jopee A fruit dessert made by the tribes of the Great Plains.

wrangler The person on a ranch or cattle drive who took care of the horses.

zoetrope or **phantascope** A device with a revolving drum used for viewing pictures that seem to move.

Zuni A Native American tribe living in what is now the state of New Mexico.

BIBLIOGRAPHY

Suzanne I. Barchers and Patricia C. Marden. *Cooking Up U.S. History: Recipes and Research to Share with Children.* Chicago: Teachers Ideas Press, 1991.

Laurie Carlson. *More Than Moccasins: A Kid's Activity Guide to Traditional North American Indian Life.* Chicago: Chicago Review Press, 1994.

Laurie Carlson. *Westward Ho! An Activity Guide to the Wild West.* Chicago: Chicago Review Press, 1996.

Cobblestone: The History Magazine for Young People. 30 Grove Street, Peterborough, NH   03458.
  The Oregon Trail, December 1981
  Children's Toys, December 1986
  America's Folk Art, August 1991

Everett Dick. *Tales of the Frontier: From Lewis and Clark to the Last Roundup.* Lincoln, NE: University of Nebraska Press, 1991.

Cheryl Edwards, Ed. *Westward Expansion: Exploration and Settlement.* Carlisle, MA: Discovery Enterprises, 1992.

John A. Garraty, Ed. *The Young Reader's Companion to American History.* Boston: Houghton Mifflin, 1994.

John Grafton. *The American West in the Nineteenth Century.* New York: Dover Publications, 1992.

Marguerite Ickic and Reba Selden Esh. *The Book of Arts and Crafts.* New York: Dover Publications, Inc., 1954.

David C. King. *The United States and Its People.* Menlo Park, CA: Addison-Wesley, 1994.

Alan and Paulette MacFarlan. *Handbook of American Indian Games.* New York: Dover Publications Inc., 1958.

Merz and Nono Minor. *The American Indian Crafts Book.* Lincoln, NE: University of Nebraska Press, 1972.

Jay Monaghan, Ed. *The Book of the American West.* New York: Julian Mesner, Inc. 1963.

Charles Phillips. *Heritage of the West.* New York: Crescent Books, 1992.

Laurence I. Seidman. *Once in the Saddle: The Cowboy's Frontier.* New York: Facts On File, 1991.

INDEX